MARCO ⊕ POLO

Munich

With Insider Tips

This travel guide was written by
Karl Forster. He was born in Lower Bavaria
and has lived in Munich for 25 years.
Forster works as a journalist on Munich's
Süddeutsche Zeitung.

marcopolo.de

The latest insider tips can be found at
www.marcopolo.de, see also page 104

MAIRS GEOGRAPHISCHER VERLAG

MARCO POLO INSIDER TIPS:
Discovered for you by our author

★ **MARCO POLO HIGHLIGHTS:**
Munich top tips at a glance

🔆 **SITES WITH A SCENIC VIEW**

🏃 **PLACES WHERE YOUNG PEOPLE
GET TOGETHER**

PRICE CATEGORIES

Hotels	
€€€	over 120 Euro
€€	60–120 Euro
€	under 60 Euro

Prices are for two people sharing a double room, including breakfast.

Restaurants	
€€€	over 12 Euro
€€	7–12 Euro
€	under 7 Euro

Prices are for a main course, drinks not included.

MAPS

[110 A1] Page numbers and coordinates for the Munich Street Atlas

[0] Site located outside map sheet

Overview map of Munich and surrounding area on pages 122–123

A plan of the S- and U-Bahn networks can be found inside back cover.

For your orientation, coordinates are also given for places which are not marked in the Street Atlas.

DID YOU KNOW?

Föhn **8** · Literary Munich **15** · Take it Easy! **29** · Top Fit! **32**
Unusual Museums **45** · Gourmet Restaurants in Munich **52**
Munich Specialities **54** · From Antiques to Junk **66**
Luxury Hotels in Munich **76** · Kunstpark Ost **83**

CONTENTS

THE BEST MARCO POLO INSIDER TIPS   Inside front cover

THE MOST IMPORTANT MARCO POLO HIGHLIGHTS   4

INTRODUCTION   7
Discover Munich!

MUNICH IN CONTEXT   13
From Football to Weisswurst

FESTIVALS AND EVENTS   16

SIGHTSEEING   19
Baths and boulevards, parks and palaces

MUSEUMS   39
I came, I saw, I was impressed!

FOOD & DRINK   49
Beer gardens, bistros and gourmet temples

SHOPPING   63
Do it in style!

ACCOMMODATION   73
Sleep well!

ENTERTAINMENT   79
Munich shines – especially at night

WALKING TOURS   91
Munich at random

OUTINGS   97
A little piece of heaven

ABSOLUTELY IN!   102

ESSENTIALS: PRACTICAL INFORMATION   103
From Banks to Time Zones

STREET ATLAS OF MUNICH WITH STREET ATLAS INDEX   107

KEY TO STREET ATLAS   109
NOTES   129
INDEX   130
PICTURE CREDITS   131

DO'S AND DON'TS   132

The Most Important
MARCO POLO Highlights

Sights and sounds you can't afford to miss

1 Starkbierzeit
High season for beer
enthusiasts. Learn how
to enjoy Lent from the
Bavarians (page 16)

2 Oktoberfest
Munich wouldn't be the
same without it (page 17)

3 Nymphenburg
All the splendour of the
Bavarian court in this palace,
museum and park (page 22)

4 Residenz
The riches of the Wittelsbach
dynasty in the Residence
Museum, Europe's most
valuable display of court
culture (page 23)

5 Frauenkirche
Sublime Gothic architecture,
lavishly and tastefully
restored after World War II
(page 25)

6 Englischer Garten
Munich's green heart
and testimony to Bavarian
Enlightenment (page 28)

7 Chinesischer Turm
Punk meets VIP and pin-
stripes meet jeans in this
beer garden. It's a classic
case of everyone to his
own taste (page 28)

Chinesischer Turm in the Englischer Garten

Tent roof on the Olympiagelände

Lenbachhaus

⭐**8** **Fernsehturm, Olympiagelände**
A must in fine weather – even more so when there's Föhn. You can see why Munich is a 'village of a million inhabitants' (page 30)

⭐**9** **Tierpark Hellabrunn**
One of the finest zoos in Europe, with many enclosures (page 31)

⭐**10** **Alte Pinakothek**
Old masters presented in a masterly setting. A paradise for lovers of fine art (page 40)

⭐**11** **Deutsches Museum**
Not just for technology freaks. Young and old lose track of time within these walls (page 42)

⭐**12** **Lenbachhaus**
Munich's most attractive gallery. The 'Blue Rider' collection is a must, even for art sceptics (page 44)

⭐**13** **Neue Pinakothek**
A 'houseful' of art from Rococo to the present day (page 45)

⭐**14** **Valentin-Karlstadt-Musäum**
Insiders breakfast here; newcomers get a lesson in open-mindedness (page 47)

⭐**15** **Kunstpark Ost**
Europe's largest nightlife complex. Will the KPO's unique combination of bars and discos be a thing of the past after 2003? (page 83)

★ *The highlights are marked on the map on the back cover*

Discover Munich!

A big-hearted metropolis with *joie de vivre* and a sense of fun. Munich embodies both traditional Bavarian and up-to-the-minute lifestyles

The Eisbach in the Englischer Garten

Munich is a city of opposites: big city and backwater, metropolis and 'village of a million inhabitants'; bastion of high-tech and *Tracht;* multiple German football champions – Bayern Munich FC – and former workers' club – TSV 1860 Munich. Munich is university and illiteracy, villas in the suburbs and inner-city broken windows, Art Nouveau and eyesores on the outskirts. Or, to put it in culinary terms, there's veal sausage and *Nouvelle Cuisine*, roast pork and truffles, beer and Bloody Mary. Munich is ambivalent, quite simply an enigma.

If you want to discover Munich, you must be prepared for a plenty of ups and downs. You have to expect both the typical grumpiness (an unmistakable sign of wanting to be left in peace) and the proverbial, friendly informality for which the average citizen of Munich is famous – off the beaten tourist track anyway. And if you observe the golden rule and take Munich at face value, then you will have a wonderful time in this city, come rain or shine, with or without 'Föhn'.

The Fischbrunnen on Marienplatz in the heart of Munich: meeting place for passers-by, musicians and demonstrators

You are, of course, free to discover Munich as you wish. We would still like to provide you with a few facts and figures nevertheless. When you think of Bavaria, you might automatically think of hills and mountains. Munich, however, is fairly flat despite its proximity to the Alps. It lies at 478 m above sea level (at the main railway station) and has a total surface area of over 310 sq km. In terms of climate, Munich is fairly cool and wet, on average, but changeable, too. So be prepared for anything, especially Munich's proverbial Föhn.

Munich is the capital of the Free State of Bavaria and the third-largest city in Germany, after Berlin and Hamburg, having more than 1.2 million inhabitants. Unemployment is well below the national average and the city claims to have the most multi-millionaires. There are still too few live music venues for young people; by contrast, high-end culture such as opera, ballet and theatre is heavily subsidised. It has an expensive underground railway network, good old-fashioned trams, 3,600 centrally-organised taxis, five daily newspapers and the Bavarian Broadcasting Corporation is the country's largest regional broadcaster. Traditionally, Munich has been governed by the Social Democrats, apart from a few brief intervals, and is therefore a 'red' stronghold in an otherwise 'black' Bavaria (black being the colour of the Christian Social Union). The city is divided into 25 districts, has 24 police stations and the highest proportion of doctors in the Republic. There are four municipal hospitals, two university teaching hospitals and numerous private clinics. Apropos of the university, Munich's 100,000 students

Metropolis and village of a million inhabitants

make it one of the largest seats of learning in Germany. Many academics have to put up with extremely high rents – here, too, Munich tops the German 'charts'.

In historical terms, Munich is at a disadvantage compared with the other Bavarian cities of Augsburg and Regensburg: it was never a Roman settlement. And yet archeological discoveries tell us that people lived here during the Neolithic period. The Celts turned up around the 6th century and four centuries later, monks decided to colonise the banks of the Tegernsee. It was that monastic settlement, 'Ze den Munichen' ('with the monks') which gave today's city its name – a fact reflected in its coat of arms, which shows the figure of a monk in his black habit, edged in gold. (Claims that the 'Münchener Kindl', the city mascot, is also clad

Föhn

An almost inexplicable phenomenon

First and foremost, Föhn is a meteorological feature which only occurs to such a marked degree along the main alpine ridge. It results when high pressure south of the Alps and low pressure north of the Alps together generate a strong, southerly wind which blows across the mountains and down into the valleys and foothills of Bavaria. It brings fine weather and astonishingly clear views – stand at the top of the Television Tower and you feel you could almost touch the mountains. There is, however, much more to Föhn than that. Secretaries spoon flour instead of coffee into coffee machines, car drivers throw all caution to the wind as if they had their own personal guardian angel on the back seat. Tolerance levels sink to an all-time low, and it has been known for Föhn to be cited as an extenuating circumstance in a criminal court case.

Beautiful people and school kids, locals and outsiders, they all come together at the beer garden

in a monk's habit are nothing more than an old, anti-clerical joke.)

In 1158, the Guelph Henry the Lion, Duke of Saxony and Bavaria, decided to outwit the Bishop of Freising. He destroyed Freising's toll bridge across the River Isar and built a new one further upstream in Ze den Munichen. Market and minting rights soon followed: Munich was founded. Thirty years later, however, Henry was outlawed and the city became the seat of the Wittelsbach dynasty (1255), whose influence can be felt to this day and whose descendants still live in the city. Here is a quick rundown of city history: in 1632, Gustavus Adolfus of Sweden conquers the city during the Thirty Years' War. Two years later, over 7,000 die of the plague, a third of the population at that

Oktoberfest and Olympia

time. The Austrians are in charge during the War of Spanish Succession, one hundred years after that, in around 1800, the French take over. A mere six years later, Bavaria becomes a kingdom with Munich as its administrative centre.

The 20th century shows Munich in a rather inglorious light. Admittedly, Kurt Eisner triggered the November Revolution here in 1918, but 1923 saw the first – failed – National Socialist coup attempt. The next one was more successful and Munich became the power base of the Nazi movement. The city was devastated by bombing during World War II.

Once more, Munich hit the headlines for all the wrong reasons. In 1972, during the Olympic Summer Games, specialist police units failed to free the Israeli hostages kidnapped by Arab terrorists – with horrifying results. Seventeen people were killed, including five hostage-takers. The cheerful and light-hearted Games were effectively over, regardless of the defiant motto: 'The games must go on'.

Munich is, thank goodness, more than just the Oktoberfest. Munich stands for a certain zest for life, and a very complex one at that. You only have to look at Munich's multitude of 'beautiful people' of both sexes. You'll find them at the disco P1, if you can get in at all, or at Pacha, the new No. 1 dance venue in town. Catch them late at the Nachtcafé, or having breakfast early in the 'morning' at 3 pm at the Forum.

At the other end of the spectrum is Munich's very own brand of Bavarian snob. He wears the traditional loden coat as if it were sable, speaks dialect with a certain detachment and a smattering of foreign words. He eats his veal sausage as if it were caviar, gives measly tips and has a season ticket for the opera.

Let's not forget the true-blue citizen of Munich. A not uncontroversial figure within the clan of the Bavarians, he is regarded with some envy. Folk out in the sticks call him somewhat scornfully a townie, or 'Stodara' in Bavarian dialect. Political cabaret artist Sigi Zimmerschied from Passau sums it up in his own inimitable style: the people of Munich are typically Bavarian in preferring to keep their mouths shut, and typically Prussian (the exact opposite) in opening them all the same!

Schafkopf and chess

That, however, is only one side of the coin – and seen from outside into the bargain. The Munich male – to make a possibly unjustified generalisation – is a quiet type. He enjoys sitting in front of his wheat beer, mulling over this and that, be it Bayern Munich or his tax return. He is not particularly outgoing, and it can be seen as a great honour if he permits a stranger to sit at the same table.

Tourists will also discover locals in the Hofbräuhaus – on display, so to speak. To meet some genuine inhabitants of Munich, it is better to try one of the smaller pubs in the side streets. Alternatively, you could stand and watch at one of the giant, open-air chess boards, in the park by the Technical University or on the Münchner Freiheit. Here, every move is hotly debated and there is scarcely a better way to get into conversation. To disturb the card players at their 'Stammtisch' is unthinkable, even if you know how to play Skat – or its Bavarian equivalent 'Schafkopf'. Not to mention 'Wattn' which involves a lot of signalling with ears, shoulders and fingers and is far too complicated for the unsuspecting foreigner.

How do the people here see their city? Towards a stranger, they would defend it tooth and nail. There is a famous battle for supremacy between the major German cities which is often fought out in the press. With monotonous regularity, certain magazines in Hamburg or newspapers in Berlin lay into the city on the Isar. In return, Munich's quills are sharpened, the poisoned arrows are primed and ready in journalistic quivers and every available weapon from the arsenal of malice is thrown into the fray. Bavarian dialect is rich in venomous terms and even the coarsest jokes can be phrased in such a way as to sound almost friendly.

Visitors are advised to leave their vehicles on the edge of town or in the hotel garage. Finding a parking space in the city centre is about as likely as finding gold at the end of the rainbow. Cars parked illegally are rigorously towed away and their owners fined heavily at the very least. And besides, Munich boasts an excellent public transport system, so why expose yourself to unnecessary hassle by driving? So, how best to get an idea of what is typical of Munich? Firstly, take it easy! Arriving by train, you should stroll through the Old Botanical Garden towards

Grumpiness and friendliness

Promenadeplatz, from there to Marienplatz, down past the Town Hall to Maximilianstrasse, northwards into Residenzstrasse and stop off at the Pfälzer Weinprobierstuben to let your first impression sink in, over a glass of wine.

To really get the feel of Munich and soak up its atmosphere, you should go to the Augustiner beer garden, behind the studios of the Bavarian Broadcasting Corporation in Arnulfstrasse. In the shade of the chestnut trees, a friendly (!) waitress will bring you a cold wheat beer and a little Bavarian delicacy to eat (how about calves' lung with bread dumplings?). The city traffic drones in the distance, but this is still an oasis of peace and contentment. No matter where you come from, New York or New Meadows, London or Littleton, you'll be glad you came.

Munich's short but splendid boulevard: Maximilianstrasse

From Football to Weisswurst

Munich's motto is 'Live and let live'

Football

Munich's two clubs in the German Bundesliga are fierce rivals. On the one hand, showy Bayern Munich FC with at most 2.4 per cent German players in the squad at any one time. On the other, the (former) workers' club TSV 1860, founded in the tough Giesing district. Both share the Olympic Stadium (as they will the scheduled new football ground). Bayern usually competes for the championship, TSV 1860 oscillates somewhere between a UEFA Cup spot and relegation. Everyone in Munich is entitled to love one club and resoundingly damn the other. Visitors are only entitled to do one thing: praise both clubs to the skies, one more than the other, depending on where they happen to be at the time. Anything else is likely to provoke the perpetration of a criminal offence – with or without Föhn.

Grumpiness

Popular culture would have us believe that the typical Bavarian is always jolly, a bit devious, even a bit stupid, but kind-hearted and,

Wheat beer and veal sausage taste even better under the Chinese Tower

despite a degree of native cunning, a good person. The truth is not quite so simple. The Bavarian (making no distinction for a change between city dwellers and country folk) is basically a grumpy, taciturn, sullen loner. He loves that special, quiet contentment which comes from being left alone to slurp his 'Mass' – that is, a litre glass of beer. He is always in the right, and if he isn't, he gets even grumpier. Non-Bavarians like to try and impress him with their wisdom, for example how to unclog a salt cellar with a toothpick. This only leaves the Bavarian cold; he prefers to unscrew the top to get at the salt.

Munich's Beer

World famous, though unjustifiably so by today's standards. Despite the fact that beer is still brewed here according to the 15th-century Bavarian purity laws (only hops, malt and water may be used), Munich's beer has lost some of its variety, to say the least. Since the already large city breweries have amalgamated, and ever more concerns from outside Bavaria are buying into them, the unique quality of local beer is no more. If you really want to enjoy a good beer, it pays to take a close look at which labels are

Treat yourself to a rather special drive around the Englischer Garten

available before choosing a restaurant. There are namely a number of small but high-quality breweries in the Munich area which produce superb beer. To give you an example, here are the three best wheat beer types: Karg (drinkable, not so fizzy), Unertl (almost oily consistency and very intense), Hopf (with a hint of banana, very refreshing). Beer from Munich is generally somewhat lighter than that from other brewing stronghold, North Rhine Westphalia. A telltale sign of a pub which is too internationally-oriented is if it serves its beer in a so-called 'Prussian Pint' which looks like a local half-litre glass, but contains only 0.4 litres – and probably costs the same as a standard half-litre. If a group of people is drinking at the same table, it is customary to clink glasses and say 'Prost!' Wheat beer experts, however, do this with the robust base of their glass. Incidentally, it's okay to wipe the froth from your mouth after the first taste.

Oktoberfest

The biggest party in the world! It took place for the first time in 1810 on the occasion of the wedding of the subsequent King Ludwig I and Princess Therese of Saxony-Hildburghausen, and featured a horse race. Today, record-breaking consumption levels of beer/victuals are measured only in millions of litres/portions. On some days, it's so crowded that the beer tents have to be closed. The current bone of contention is whether or not Munich's high society should be allowed to reserve half a tent for themselves, while the average visitor has to wait outside. Traditionally, young people, especially from Down Under, like to meet in the Hofbräu tent for drinking contests, during which the occasional discarded bra has been known to fly through the air. Why the Oktoberfest largely takes place in September (only the third and final weekend is actually in October) is one of the great mysteries of mankind.

Tracht

They really are quite a sight, the genuine Bavarian traditional costumes or 'Trachten'. The men wear short, two-buttoned buckskin knee breeches with wide, embroidered braces, collarless linen shirts, knee-length socks, 'Haferlschuhe' (a type of brogue) and a felt hat crowned with a *Gamsbart*, a tuft of hair from a chamois goat. The ladies wear a dress called a 'Dirndl', with a figure-hugging bodice and apron. These are embellished individually, according to place of origin. Munich itself has no traditional costume of its own. The locals favour a loosely Bavarian style with a casual, woollen jacket or thick, waterproof loden coat.

Weisswurst

A traditional Munich second breakfast of veal sausage with wheat beer instead of coffee. Ordered singly, not in pairs, they consist largely of veal sausage meat, water and other secret ingredients, should be heated gently in water (otherwise the skin will burst) and served with sweet mustard and a pretzel. The correct eating technique is a matter for the most heated discussion. The layman cuts it in half lengthways and cuts out the meat at random. The would-be, dyed-in-the-wool Bavarian (usually an outsider) prefers the handed-down technique of taking the sausage in one hand, dipping it in the mustard and, having bitten the end off, sucking out the contents! The expert, however, spears it, cuts it three-quarters of the way along and turns it elegantly inside out (works only with a perfectly-heated sausage). They used to say that a veal sausage should never hear the clock strike noon, because that would mean it was too old to eat. Luckily, thanks to modern-day conservation methods, this is no longer a problem.

Litarary Munich

Tips for bookworms

An attractive city like Munich will naturally be reflected in both serious and trivial literature. Thomas Mann's masterly novella *Gladius Dei* of 1902 delivered a well-worn and generally wrongly-cited quotation about this glittering metropolis: 'München leuchtete' (Munich glowed). Mann, with fellow German literary giants Rainer Maria Rilke, Hermann Hesse and his brother Heinrich Mann, contributed to the early 20th-century satirical magazine, *Simplicissimus,* a last literary high point before the slump into nationalistic tones between the wars. History fans might like to read *The White Rose: Munich 1942–1943* (Ingo Scholl and Dorothee Sölle), and *One Day in September. The Story of the 1972 Munich Olympics Massacre* (Simon Reeve). On a lighter note, *The Beer Drinker's Guide to Munich* (Larry Hawthorne) might also come in handy.

Festivals and Events

Five seasons, festivals and the biggest knees up in the world

The celebration curve is markedly defined by tradition and has two highlights which both are connected with beer. The so-called 'Strong Beer

Roll out the barrel on the Wiesn!

or Fifth Season' in which a specially-brewed strong beer is served up, and of course the world-famous Oktoberfest. The 'Strong Beer Season' is more of an internal affair, while the Oktoberfest invites the whole world to join in.

Public Holidays:

1 January New Year's Day; **6 January** Epiphany; **Good Friday; Easter Monday; 1 May** Labour Day; **Ascension Day; Whit Monday; Corpus Christi; 15 August** Assumption; **3 October** Unification Day; **1 November** All Saints' Day; **25 and 26 December** Christmas. On Carnival Thursday some shops stay closed, on Carnival Tuesday all of them do. Many shops also close on All Souls' Day (2 Nov). On 24 Dec and 31 Dec shops close at lunchtime. Shops closed on Sundays are also closed on public holidays.

Festivals and Events

January/February

Carnival: Carnival Thursday is traditionally ladies' day – men, watch those ties! On Carnival Sunday, the (female) market stall-holders dance on the Viktualien-markt. Every seven years, traditional Cooper's Dance.

March/April

★ *Strong Beer Season:* Two weeks after Ash Wednesday until Easter, because in 1651 the Paulaner monks decided that fasting went down better with beer than without it.

Easter Sunday: Easter egg hunt at Hellabrunn Zoo (with 10,000 hidden eggs).

Ballet Festival: One week in March at the Bavarian State Opera *(Bayerische Staatsoper; P. O. Box 10 01 48; 80075 Munich; Fax 089-21 85 19 03).*

Spring Festival: Mini-Oktoberfest on the Theresienwiese, two weeks at the end of April

June–August

Munich International Film Festival in June: Directors from all over the world show the latest film trends. Party with the stars in the evening. Tickets: *Tel. 089-48 09 06 98 or www.filmfest-muenchen.de*

Opera Festival in June and July: Tickets are hard to come by, advance booking from end of January *(Bayerische Staatsoper; P. O. Box 10 01 48; 80075 Munich; Fax 089-21 85 19 03).* The supporting programme *festspiel +* is generally more interesting.

Insider Tip *Tollwood Summer Festival:* Three weeks in June/July at the Olympic Park (south). Large culture and market festival with around 100 musical and theatrical events attracting some one million visitors *(Tickets: Tel. 0700-38 38 50 24 or www.tollwood.de).*

Schleissheim Palace Concerts: High-quality programme of Baroque and classical music in a wonderful setting, generally from June to August.

Insider Tip *Rock Summer in the Theatron:* Throughout August, every afternoon and evening, the local and regional rock scene gets together at the Olympic Lake.

September/October

★ *Oktoberfest:* Over four weekends, the last being the first in October. Beer festival and funfair, the biggest party in the world.

November/December

Insider Tip *Tollwood Winter Festival:* During Advent, Munich's prettiest Christmas Market, on the Theresienwiese, including the usually superb En-Suite cultural programme (until 31 Dec).

April/July/October

Auer Dult: Three times a year, for nine days at a time, Munich's biggest flea market; Saturday before 1 May, Saturday after St Jacob's Day in July and third Saturday in October; *Mariahilfplatz; bus: 52, 56*

At the Tollwood Summer Festival

Baths and boulevards, parks and palaces

A flying visit would not do justice to Munich – its beauty and variety have to be experienced and appreciated at leisure

If you want not just to see Munich but to take a really close look at the city, remember this: 'Take your time!' To get more than merely a superficial impression, you have to be prepared to let Munich's many delightful details sink in gradually and, above all, regard them in the context of surroundings, history and people.

There are so many different things to see and experience, it's difficult to know where to set priorities, or even where to get started! It makes no sense trying to 'do' the entire Munich Residence in two days. An evening in the Fountain Court listening to a classical concert in summer; an afternoon of rock at the Theatron in the Olympic Park; an early morning visit to the stall-holders on the Viktualienmarkt; a trip to Nymphenburg Park with an expert biologist at your side; a wedding at the Theatinerkirche late on a Saturday – that's Munich.

Baroque and Rococo at its finest: walk in the footsteps of princes in the park at Schloss Nymphenburg

View from the tower of the Peterskirche

ARCHITECTURAL HIGHLIGHTS

Altes Rathaus [111 D4]

A tip for lovers: the bronze *Julia* on the south side of the over 500-year-old Old Town Hall is your patron saint. It is a popular belief that you can curry her favour by giving her flowers. The building has often been badly damaged and, after World War II was re-built with little regard for its original appearance. The ballroom features impressive wooden barrel vaulting and is still the setting for prestigious events. The famous Morris Dancers, however, are copies; the originals are in the Munich City Museum. Access to tower: *Mon–Thurs 9 am–4 pm, Fri 9 am–1 pm, Sat 10 am–5 pm; S- and U-Bahn: Marienplatz*

Bavaria-Filmgelände [0]

★ A must for visitors with children: 'Hollywood on the Isar'. The 3.5-sq-km site, to the southwest, between the city and Grünwald, has seen German film history in the making since 1919. The celluloid greats have worked here: Orson Welles, Alfred Hitchcock, Billy Wilder. Gina Lollobrigida stood in front of the cameras here, as did the likes of Liz Taylor or Romy Schneider. The guided tour of the Bavaria Film Studios includes a visit to the model of the submarine used in Wolfgang Petersen's film *Das Boot*

Modern Munich: Hypobank Tower

plus a look at the animated characters out of *The Never-Ending Story* and *E. T.* There is also a special VIP Tour (dates and times on request), which offers special insights into life on the film set, with demonstrations of stunts, special effects and even the occasional meeting with local film stars. *1 Mar–3 Nov: daily 9 am–4 pm; 4 Nov–28 Feb: daily 10 am–3 pm; Tel. 64 99 23 04; Bavariafilmplatz 7; www.filmstadt. de; tram: 25*

Verwaltungsgebäude HYPO-Vereinsbank [115 F6]

Apart from the BMW clover-leaf-shaped office block, the 'Hypobank Tower', headquarters of the HYPO-Vereinsbank, is the only serious architectural addition to the Munich skyline since the Olympic Park. To call it 'Munich's only skyscraper' at a height of 114 m (a third of the Olympic Tower) is a bit of an overstatement. Added to that, the office block stands outside the central ring road – to the credit of the urban planners – that is, outside the city centre. Architect Betz and company have managed, with this complex of prism-shaped structures 'strapped' to massive columns, to set new standards in a city otherwise lacking modern architectural features. *Arabellastrasse 12; U-Bahn: 4, Arabellapark*

Maximilianeum [119 D2]

In the exuberant spirit of the 19th century, Maximilian II wanted to erect a genuine 'Acropolis' at the end of Maximilianstrasse. Architect Friedrich Bürklein fulfilled his wish. Originally, it provided accommodation and teaching facilities for highly talented Bavarian school pupils; it still subsidises board and lodging for top grade students during their studies to this day. In 1949, the Bavarian State Government and Free State Senate moved in. By law, any citizen may sit in on public sessions, though visitors are advised to phone in advance to find out the times of guided tours. *Tel. 412 60; U-Bahn: 4/5, Max-Weber-Platz*

Müllersches Volksbad [119 D3]

★ Even if you don't feel like a refreshing swim, the beautiful Art-Nouveau building is worth seeing for its own sake. The vaulted roofs above both pools, the steam bath and tiled sauna in this magnificent building on the Isar deserve an extended visit. *Rosenheimer Strasse 1; Tel. 23 61 34 34; S-Bahn: Rosenheimer Platz; tram: 18*

The Müllersches Volksbad: an Art-Nouveau gem

Nationaltheater [111 E3]

At the beginning of the 19th century, Bavaria's first king, Maximilian I Joseph, commissioned the young Karl von Fischer with the building of a theatre in the style of the Odéon in Paris. The project was ill-fated from the start. A mere five years after its official opening in 1818, a huge fire destroyed the majestic, Classicist building. Leo von Klenze set about reconstructing the theatre, under the suspicious gaze of the people. Many were convinced that it had been an act of blasphemy in the first place to build a profane temple of the arts on a site where Franciscan monks had once been active.

World War II also took its toll on the building. Von Klenze's work was virtually razed to the ground. Instead of agreeing to a modern replacement, however, the city fathers – with the approval of the Free State – decided on a renewed reconstruction of the Classicist structure. Today, Max-Joseph-Platz is dominated by the memorial to the King and the Greek colonnaded portico of the theatre with its staggered double gable. The magnificent auditorium only holds an audience of some 2,100, less for example than the small Circus Krone. For this reason, each seat has to be subsidised to the tune of 100 Euro per performance, in order to maintain the standard of productions, also a target for fierce criticism. The more recent history of the theatre has been perfectly respectable. Richard Strauss conducted numerous premieres here; conductors such as Clemens Krauss, Bruno Walter, Hans Knappertsbusch (known affectionately to his students as 'Knaa'), Solti, Fricsay and Keilberth laid the foundations of their illustrious careers within these walls. Two figures, by no means friends, had a decisive influence on the repertoire and standard of this world-famous house in the 1980s: theatre director August Everding, who died in 1999, and chief musical director Wolfgang Sawallisch. Zubin Mehta is the current chief conductor. The high point of the season is the Opera Festival in July. *Guided tours by arrangement; Tel. 21 85 10 21; Max-Joseph-Platz 2; U-Bahn: 3/4/5/6, Odeonsplatz*

Neues Rathaus [111 D4]

◁▷ Built between 1867 and 1908, the New Town Hall is pompous rather than being of real value in terms of cultural history. An excessive enthusiasm for all things Gothic inspired architect Georg von Hauberrisser from Graz in Austria. Below the 80-m-high tower, Europe's fourth largest *Glockenspiel* (carillon) is located in an oriel window. Every day at 11 am (from May to October also at noon and 5 pm) it tells the story of two major events which took place on Marienplatz: the tournament to celebrate the wedding of Duke William V of Bavaria and Renata of Lorraine (1568), and the Cooper's Dance in remembrance of the plague in 1517 and repeated every seven years since, at Carnival time. (Next performance: 2005.) *Tower lift in summer: Mon–Thurs 9 am–4 pm, Fri 9 am–1 pm; S- and U-Bahn: Marienplatz*

Nymphenburg [112 A4–5]

★ They certainly knew how to give presents in the days of Elector Ferdinand Maria. At that time, in the mid-17th century, Henriette Adelaide gave birth to the Elector's long-awaited son and heir Max Emanuel. In return, the proud father presented her with Nymphenburg Palace. The façade of this Baroque building, constructed between 1664 and 1757, is around 700 m long, three times as long as the Olympic Stadium. It served the Bavarian rulers as a summer residence, and as you walk through the magnificent apartments, you can imagine the extravagant life led here during the golden age of the Bavarian court. In addition to the central building with its splendid Stone Hall and stunning Gallery of Beauties (a group of 38 attractive Munich ladies who enjoyed varying degrees of intimacy with Ludwig I), the *Marstallmuseum* (Royal Stables Museum) has the world's finest collection of carriages, sledges and harness, dating back to the days of the Bavarian Electors and Kings. The *Porzellanmuseum* (Porcelain Museum) contains valuable pieces from the Nymphenburg factory.

Also worth a visit are the *Schlosspark* (park) with its hothouses, the *Amalienburg,* a prime example of courtly Rococo, the *Badenburg* with its Chinese wallpaper, the *Pagodenburg's* then fashionable Chinese furnishings and the *Magdalenenklause,* which Elector Max Emanuel had built in later life as a meditation chapel. *Admission: 7.50 Euro; combined ticket 'Staatliche Museen und Sammlungen' is valid for 14 days and costs 15 Euro; Apr–15 Oct: daily 9 am–6 pm, Thurs 9 am–8 pm; 16 Oct–Mar: daily 10 am–4 pm; U-Bahn: 1, Rotkreuzplatz; tram: 17; bus: 41*

Residenz [111 E2–3]

★ This is an ideal place to learn about the history of Bavaria and the Wittelsbach dynasty. The Munich Residence impresses the visitor with its overwhelming grandeur. We recommend planning at least a whole day for a visit. Following the bomb damage of World War II, the Free State has poured millions into the restoration of the 'cultural heart' of Bavaria, which for 500 years was the seat of its rulers. Every architectural style which constitutes Bavarian cultural history is on display here: austere Renaissance, extravagant Baroque, dainty Rococo down to linear Classicism. In 1385 the foundation stone was laid for the 'Neuveste' (new castle) in the northeast of the old city. Over the centuries, the Residence grew bit by bit – although progress was interrupted by fires – into the three main complexes and six inner courtyards of the present day.

If you haven't enough time to look at all the treasures between Residenzstrasse, Hofgartenstrasse and Marstallstrasse, you should at least visit the *Residenzmuseum* **Insider Tip** (Residence Museum) with Europe's most precious examples of court culture. The vestibule, ancestral portrait gallery, porcelain collection, Antiquarium (in which the Minister President still holds receptions), the porcelain chambers, the 'Reiches Zimmer', Mirror Room and the Nibelungen Halls provide a general overview. *Fri–Wed 9 am–6 pm, Thurs 9 am–8 pm; Max-Joseph-Platz 3; S- and U-Bahn: Marienplatz; tram: 19/27/29*

MARCO POLO **Highlights** »Sightseeing«

★ **Asamkirche**
Breathtaking Baroque
(page 24)

★ **Fernsehturm, Olympiagelände**
A Föhnomenal experience
not to be missed (page 30)

★ **Glockenbachviertel**
Insider Tip An off-beat Munich beauty
(page 31)

★ **Nymphenburg**
Wittelsbach pomp and
circumstance (page 22)

★ **Residenz**
Bavaria's cultural heart
(page 23)

★ **Müllersches Volksbad**
Insider Tip Munich's most desirable
property includes sauna
and Turkish bath (page 21)

★ **Tierpark Hellabrunn**
Unbearably good (page 31)

★ **Frauenkirche**
Trademark of the city
(page 25)

★ **Bavaria-Filmgelände**
Take a dive in the 'Das Boot'
sub (page 20)

★ **Englischer Garten and Chinesischer Turm**
Cold beer in a green oasis
(page 28)

Südfriedhof [118 A4]

A paradise for history fans. The South Cemetery was established in the 16th century. Albrecht V intended it for use as a burial ground for the poor. In the 17th century it served as a plague cemetery and in the 18th century was Munich's main cemetery. Following its extension in the mid-19th century, it became the preferred resting place of many famous citizens.

A stroll between the gravestones gives a highly personal insight into the history of the city. Among others, sculptor Roman Anton Boos (St Peter's Church), architect Friedrich von Gärtner (Field Marshall's Hall), historical painter Wilhelm von Kaulbach, architect Leo von Klenze and the painter of *The Poor Poet*, Carl Spitzweg, are laid to rest here. *Thalkirchner Strasse 17; U-Bahn: 1/2/3/6, Sendlinger Tor*

Universität [114 C6]

The Ludwig-Maximilian University (Ludwig I moved it in 1826 from Landshut to Munich) with its 60,000 students is, after the Free University of Berlin, Germany's second-largest. Names such as those of scientists Fraunhofer and Röntgen, philosopher Schelling and sociologist Max Weber are synonymous with the University, and have given their names to streets in the city. On either side of Ludwigstrasse are the two bowl-shaped fountains, much prized at home and abroad, not only among the students. The western building is in the neo-Romanesque style, the former seminary to the east seems more distant and restrained. The university's official home, 'Geschwister-Scholl-Platz', was named in remembrance of Sophie and Hans Scholl. As members of the 'White Rose' group, they were executed in 1943 for resisting the Hitler regime. *Geschwister-Scholl-Platz; U-Bahn: 3/6, Universität*

CHURCHES

Asamkirche [110 C5]

★ Martyr Johannes von Nepomuk is the patron saint of bridges. Surprisingly, the church consecrated in his name is around one kilometre away from the Isar. For all that, St Nepomuk has a task to fulfil: the Asamkirche in Sendlinger Strasse, flanked by chic boutiques and shops, represents an ideological and architectural bridge between two worlds, as is so typical of Munich. Zest for life and blatant consumerism come up against tradition and deeply-rooted Catholicism, modern, functional architecture against magnificent, extravagant Baroque. For amateur photographers, the beautiful, subdued lighting inside the church is a real challenge; for fans of art history, the four winding columns which frame the high altar and the sculpted representation of the Trinity above it invite limitless interpretation. Between 1975 and 1982, the church underwent costly renovation – so costly that vicious tongues asserted the entire city council could have bought its place in Paradise for the amount spent. *Sendlinger Strasse 32; U-Bahn: 1/3/6/2, Sendlinger Tor*

Bürgersaalkirche [110 B3]

Historically of interest due to its role as former meeting place of the 'Marian Congregation', a religious

Baroque splendour inside the Asamkirche

group of priests and laymen close to the Jesuits. In the crypt is the burial place of Father Rupert Mayer, one of the role models of the Munich resistance movement against Hitler. He was beatified by Pope John Paul II. The Baroque prayer chamber on the upper floor has been beautifully restored. The figures of the guardian angels above the organ gallery are by Ignatz Günther. *Neuhauser Strasse 47; S- and U-Bahn: Stachus*

Dreifaltigkeitskirche [110 C2–3]

Munich's first, late-Baroque church was founded in typically Bavarian fashion. Valet's daughter Anna Maria Lindtmayr was so overwhelmed with visions of impending doom for the city in the forefront of the brutal War of Spanish Succession, that she dedicated herself to the building of a church to assuage the wrath of God and spare her city. Citizens and representatives of the rural population were so impressed that they commissioned Italian architect and court master builder Giovanni Antonio Viscardi with the building of the Holy Trinity Church. The unconventional interior, with its oblique columns and Cosmas Damian Asam's magnificent ceiling fresco, unites Italian vigour with Bavarian expressiveness. *Pacelli-strasse 6; S- and U-Bahn: Stachus*

Frauenkirche [111 D3]

★ ◁◁ Its proper name is the Cathedral Church of Our Lady and it is the Episcopal church of the archdiocese of Munich-Freising. Longer than a football pitch (109 m), it holds 2,000 worshippers and, with its twin bulbous domes atop the towers, is the true symbol of the city – more so than Bayern Munich FC. The 99-m-high southern tower is one metre shorter than the other, and thanks to an old law prohibiting the obstruction of the view, both can be seen almost from the southern and western city boundaries. The late-Gothic structure impresses most because of its clear, austere layout. Opinions are divided as to whether the restoration of the three naves during the 1970s can be considered a success. However, renovation work on the interior completed in 1994 has won universal praise. In any case, the visitor will find a wealth of ecclesiastical treasures, for example the richly-decorated monument to Emperor Ludwig of Bavaria. An ascent of the tower is an essential part of any visit. *South tower (98 m) open Apr–Oct: Mon–Sat 10am–5 pm; Frauenplatz 1; S- and U-Bahn: Marienplatz*

Heiliggeistkirche [111 E4]

Together with the Church of Our Lady and St Peter's Church, the Church of the Holy Spirit is one of Munich's oldest places of worship, probably built in 1208 as a Romanesque chapel. It was rebuilt in the Gothic style in 1327 after a great fire and later given a Baroque face-lift by the Asam brothers. Almost completely destroyed in World War II, it has been painstakingly restored over many years. The 19th-century neo-Baroque façade is the dominant external feature of Rosentalgasse. *Tal 77; S- and U-Bahn: Marienplatz*

Herz-Jesu-Kirche [112 C5]

Burnt down in 1994, the Herz-Jesu-Kirche in Neuhausen was redesigned by architects Allmann, Sattler and Wappner. Their daring glass structure in a shimmering blue tone was at first rejected by the more conservative residents in the district, but has since gained a reputation as a symbol of modern Catholic thought. It is the venue for high-quality concerts and exhibitions. *Romanstrasse 6; U-Bahn: 1, Rotkreuzplatz*

Ludwigskirche [114 C6]

Immediately recognisable as a Romanesque-Classicist reproduction (by Gärtner), the church contains a particularly valuable artefact: one of the largest frescos in the world, painted behind and above the altar, the *Last Judgement* by Peter Cornelius (intended to rival Michelan-

gelo's in the Sixtine Chapel). The two towers contrast markedly with the imposing Theatinerkirche to the south. *Ludwigstrasse 20; U-Bahn: 3/6, Universität*

Michaelskirche [110 C3]

Never at a loss when it came to self-promotion, Duke William V wished to create an imposing monument to the Counter Reformation with the building of this church, and in so doing almost bankrupted the state. He could later credit himself with the construction – for 'his Jesuits' – of the second-largest barrel-vaulted church in the world, after St Peter's in Rome, a structural miracle by the standards of the day. Today's façade, though magnificent, blends obligingly into the overall architectural picture of Neuhauser Strasse. The crypt contains the graves of a number of Bavarian rulers, including Ludwig II. *Neuhauser Strasse 52; S- and U-Bahn: Stachus*

Peterskirche [111 D4]

◣◢ One of Munich's oldest buildings, known as 'Old Peter'. Long before the founding of the city, a chapel stood on the 'Petersbergl' hill. Over the centuries, an architecturally interesting combination of Romanesque, Gothic, early Baroque and Rococo elements has developed, which entices many – not just Catholic – visitors, especially on Sundays and public holidays, to listen to the wonderful Mozart and Haydn masses. During the week, too, the church is a peaceful oasis amidst the bustle of the inner city, and boasts a wealth of precious objects by such craftsmen as Erasmus Grasser (marble slabs), Nikolaus Gottfried Stuber (high altar) and Ignaz Günther (sedile to the right of the altar and the Mariahilf Altar in the southern nave). *Tower open: Mon–Sat 9 am–6 pm, Sun 10.15 am–6 pm; Rindermarkt 1; S- and U-Bahn: Marienplatz*

St Anna im Lehel [118 C2]

Not only one of its most significant, but Bavaria's first Rococo church. Badly damaged in World War II, it has been beautifully restored. It was begun in 1727 by Johann Michael Fischer and took five years to complete. Fischer introduced a new architectural feature, the oval-shaped interior. The Asam brothers contributed the decorative frescos in the vaulted roof and the altarpieces, which have been painstakingly reconstructed. *St-Anna-Platz; U-Bahn: 4/5, Lehel*

Theatinerkirche [111 D2]

The birth of Max Emanuel must have greatly impressed his parents, Elector Ferdinand Maria and Henriette Adelaide. Not only did papa present mama with Schloss Nymphenburg upon his heir's birth, but the couple gratefully commissioned one of Munich's fine churches and dedicated it to St Cajetan, the founder of the Theatine Order. Since the saint and the order both originated in Italy, the architecture echoes the elegant Italian high-Baroque style. Some one hundred years after the laying of the foundation stone, François Cuvilliés completed its Rococo façade. The Theatine Church is, together with St Ludwig's Church and the Church of Our Lady, one of the most striking features of the Munich skyline. Particularly impressive are its barrel-vaulted construction, the cross-ing cupola, the high altar with its depiction of the Madonna by Rubens pupil Caspar de Crayer, the exquisitely fashioned black pulpit and the imposing royal crypt of the Wittelsbach dynasty underneath the high altar. *Theatinerstrasse 22; U-Bahn: 3/4/5/6, Odeonsplatz*

PARKS & GARDENS

Botanischer Garten [112 A4]

The 20-ha Botanical Garden to the north of Nymphenburg Park rates not just with biologists and botanists as one of the finest gardens in Europe. All year round, beauty and science combine in per-

The elegance of Italian high Baroque: Theatinerkirche

fect harmony to delight amateur photographers and flower lovers alike. Whether in the formal garden, the genetics department, the Alpine House, the rhododendron grove or the arboretum, the splendour of nature is on display. From medicinal plants to insect-eating flowers, the explanatory material on all the exhibits is informative without being too scholarly. *Daily 9 am–6 pm; in winter until 5 pm; hothouses: 9 am–11.45 am, 1 pm–5.30 pm; in winter until 4 pm only; Menzinger Strasse 65; U-Bahn: 1, Rotkreuzplatz; tram: 17*

Englischer Garten [115 D–F 1–6]
★ New York has its Central Park, London its Hyde Park, but no one in Munich would swap 'his' English Garden for either of them. Conceived in 1788 in the spirit of the Enlightenment by physicist and lieutenant-general of the Bavarian army Sir Benjamin Thompson, Earl of Rumford, it was laid out by Elector Karl Theodor a year later. Admittedly, the 5-km-long and up to 1-km-wide park is today perhaps more famous for its aficionados of nude bathing. The people of Munich, however, tend to ignore such minor disparities on their way to the Chinese Tower, to the Kleinhesselohe Lake or to the Aumeister beer garden. The English Garden changes in character as you progress northwards, becoming wilder, lonelier, more overgrown. The classic features (and meeting points): *Monopteros* in the south, not far from the Haus der Kunst, a Classicist round temple designed by architect Leo von Klenze. This is where the young people of the world (and the young-at-heart) get together to play music – carefully observed by the police, especially the drug squad. The meadow in front is a magnet for dog-owners and all manner of four-legged friends. Above the ice-cold arm of the Isar, the 'Eisbach', is the ★ *Chinesische Turm* (Chinese Tower, 1790) which burnt down in 1944 and was rebuilt in 1951. At its base is Munich's most famous beer garden. One kilometre further north, before the central ring road, a fine

Eisbach surfers in the Englischer Garten

Take it Easy!

Roman baths, oriental massage and that Caribbean feeling

The *Mathildenbad (Mathildenstrasse 5; Tel. 55 45 73; Sun–Thurs noon–1 am, Fri&Sat noon–3 am; U-Bahn: 1/2/3/6, Sendlinger Tor)* is a hot tip for those who deserve a real treat. All-over mud packs, Turkish steam bath, oriental massage, in short, the best of Ottoman bathing culture. There's also a sauna, a bio sauna with light therapy, all in fabulous, marble and mosaic surroundings. Or have a relaxing day out at the *Therme in Erding (Thermenallee 1; Tel. 08122-22 99 22; Mon–Fri 10 am–11 pm, Sat&Sun 9 am–11 pm; MVV-Kombiticket: 14 Euro for 4 hours incl. return trip: S-Bahn: 6, Erding)*. One of the most attractive indoor and outdoor swimming pools in Bavaria. Drilling for oil, engineers hit upon a thermal spring, and this luxurious multi-function bathing centre was built instead.

restaurant with beer garden sits alongside the *Kleinhesseloher See* (Kleinhesselohe Lake) in a house built by Gabriel von Seidl in 1883. Only half an hour's walk further on towards Freimann, lies the *Aumeister*, an old inn built for huntsmen, with its beautiful garden. A seat in the shade of its trees is an ideal spot in the summer heat. Unfortunately we have to warn against walking here at night. *U-Bahn: 3/6, Gisela-strasse or Universität*

Insider Tip

Hofgarten [111 E1–2]

The former Royal Garden is also Munich's most recent bone of contention. In 1988, the then Bavarian Chancellor Franz Josef Strauss attempted to build himself a memorial here in the form of a gigantic state chancellery building. The general public however, supported by architects, environmentalists and municipal politicians, campaigned vehemently against the 'Strausso-

leum'. Although his successor Max Streibl reduced the plans to an acceptable size, the overall picture of the Italianate-style garden is much disturbed by the structure which was built around the cupola of the ruined Army Museum. *U-Bahn: 3/4/5/6, Odeonsplatz*

Luitpoldpark [114 B2–3]

Munich's citizens knew how to behave towards a Prince Regent. To mark Prince Luitpold's 90th birthday, in 1911, 90 lime trees were planted in a park named after him in the west of Schwabing. Today, the park is a favourite inner-city recreation ground. A pleasant stroll takes you from here to the Olympic Park or you can stop off at the *Bamberger Haus* with its small brewery which is run by Luitpold's successor, Prince Luitpold from the 'Schlossbrauerei Kaltenberg'. Bamberg House is the venue for exhibitions of works by famous caricatur-

Insider Tip

Daring and seemingly weightless: the famous roof at the Olympia Park

ists and cartoonists. *U-Bahn: 2/3, Scheidplatz*

Olympiagelände [113 E–F 2–3]
Munich's *Olympiapark* (Olympic Park) is synonymous world-wide with revolutionary contemporary architecture. When the city was awarded the Summer Games of 1972, the local authorities decided to drive home the Games' message of cheerful competition even before they began. Architects Behnisch and Partners went for the archaic construction principle of the tent. On the 3-sq-km site of the former royal Bavarian military training grounds at Oberwiesenfeld they erected a complex of sporting facilities, joined thematically and physically by a series of daring, tent-like roof structures which are dwarfed by the 290-m-high ★ ◥↙ *Fernsehturm* (Television Tower). The lifts are in operation from 9 am to midnight and the decent restaurant, which rotates on its own axis once an hour, is also open at this time. Centrepoint of the Olympic Park is the *Stadium* which seats 70,000. Be sure to take a look at it before it possibly falls into disuse. Football clubs Bayern Munich and TSV 1860 are currently building themselves a new ground in Fröttmaning on the motorway to Nuremberg. The so-called Allianz Arena – also known as 'The Toilet Bowl' – is to be ready in time for football's World Cup in 2006, which is to be hosted by Germany. No one is quite sure what will then happen to the multi-purpose Olympic Stadium. Free pop concerts take place in the summer at the *Theatron* by the Olympic Lake. The *Olympic Hill*, a pile of

rubble heaped up after World War II, gets joggers sweating and gives the more relaxed visitor a fine view over the city.

Tierpark Hellabrunn [0]

★ The impressive zoo lies on a triangular site on the Isar meadows between Harlachinger Berg and the landing stage of the Isar canal. Hellabrunn boasts 4,000 animals, many of them born here, and prides itself on giving them as much freedom of movement as possible. The father of the German circus tradition, Carl Hagenbeck, decided to organise the zoo according to continents instead of species. Hence, in the north, you'll find bison from North America, in the south, Edmi gazelle from Africa and to the west, the Barasinghta deer from Asia. *Apr–Sept: 8 am–6 pm; Oct–Mar: 9 am–5 pm; Tierparkstrasse 30; U-Bahn: 3, Thalkirchen; bus: 52, Tierpark*

Westpark [116 B–C4]

South of the old exhibition centre, this 7-sq-km recreational park was completed in 1983, the year in which Munich hosted the fourth International Horticultural Exhibition. The park is bisected by Garmischer Strasse.

In summer, various open-air cultural events are staged around the lake. West of this stands the original wooden pagoda built for the exhibition by 200 Nepalese craftsmen. *U-Bahn: 6, Westpark*

URBAN DISTRICTS

Gärtnerplatzviertel [111 D6]

Munich's gay and lesbian scene has established itself here, thanks to a number of pioneering individuals who fought doggedly for their rights. The district around the Gärtnerplatz has become more open. You'll find not only the highest proportion of hairdressers in the city, but a colourful selection of pubs. Some publicans are just out to make a fast buck, other places exude a warm, student-type atmosphere. Proprietors change fast here, though, so just go along and see for yourself!

Glockenbachviertel [118 A4–5]

★ Named after the stream which flows past the old South Cemetery. The area between the Schlachthof (slaughterhouse) district, Gärtnerplatz district and the inner city has developed its own highly original atmosphere. Artists from the Glockenbachwerkstatt, actors from the theatres around Hans-Sachs-Strasse – also the location of Munich's only button-hole shop – populate the lively pub scene. Here you can hear classical music – also live. At Jupiter-Sinfonie, listen to Mozart with your café au lait at Holzstrasse 41. The tide of redevelopment is only slowly advancing on the district – a good place to linger for a while.

Haidhausen [119 D3–4]

Paris, Orléans, Metz, Gravelotte, Bazeilles – these street names have earned this district between the Isar and the Ostbahnhof, Bogenhausen and Au the nickname 'French Quarter'. They may sound harmless, but they hark back to the blood-ridden days of the Franco-Prussian War (1870–71), a tribute to the victorious Bavarian Corps. In the years after the 'economic miracle' of the 1950s, Haidhausen was popularly re-christened 'Little Naples' or 'Istanbul on the Isar' – due to the number of immigrant workers. Then, the real disaster struck: a veritable invasion of Schwabing residents began. Tired of their own district, they came to Haidhausen and brought with them their discos and bistros, boutiques and swindlers. Today, Haidhausen glitters; the main thoroughfares at least. Take some time to wander through the narrow side streets and courtyards, searching in the little shops for curios and other knick-knacks, and you will sense the charm of this district, which, despite the monolithic concrete Gasteig Culture Centre and the giant City Hilton Hotel, has managed to retain its identity.

Neuhausen/   **[112–113**
Nymphenburg/Gern   **B–E 3–5]**

West of the central ring road begins Munich's up-market neighbour-hood. The beautiful houses date back largely to the turn of the 20th century, and in some cases have been in the same family for genera-tions. It is well worth taking a walk through the narrow streets, say, from Volkartstrasse via Orffstrasse and Ruffinistrasse, and not just because of the architecture. Here, peace and tranquillity are the order of the day. Unfortunately the Rotkreuzplatz is a prime example of urban planning gone wrong, and the ugly Red-Cross Hospital build-ing is a real blot on the landscape. The infrastructure, however, is in-tact. There are still tiny household goods shops in which screws are sold by weight, and fruit and vege-table stalls on squares and pave-ments. Further westwards, in the direction of Nymphenburg Palace, the houses become bigger and grander. Towards Dantebad lies one of the city's finest beer gardens, the Taxisgarten with its legendary *spareribs*.

Inside Tip

Top Fit!

Sport in Munich – either go up the wall or run for it!

Climbing freaks will find one of the largest indoor climbing centres in Europe in Thalkirchnerstrasse at the district sports centre. The German Alpine Club has its *climbing centre here (daily 9 am–11 pm; Thalkirchnerstrasse 207; Tel. 22 15 91; U-Bahn: 3, Brudermühlstrasse)*, where clever red-point aces train. A total of 18 m of climbing walls, 150 routes, and degrees of difficulty from 3 to 10 mean there's something for everyone. The *English Garden* is a jogger's paradise. A complete circuit round the outside is just under 20 km. Ideal starting point is the *car park* at the *Aumeister beer garden* in the north, as it's quieter here; in the south, there are more people out walking. Other great jogging routes: *Nymphen-burg Park, Westpark* and *Olympic Park* (get up that hill!).

Schlachthofviertel [117 F5]

The district has so far managed to hold on to its almost rural character, especially around Dreimühlenstrasse. Even today, in summer, you can smell the abattoir ('Schlachthof') which gives the district its name. Here, between Kapuzinerstrasse and the wholesale market (Europe's biggest), Goethestrasse and Isar, there are any number of original pubs selling supposedly the best veal sausages in Munich.

Top of the list is the *Wirtshaus im Schlachthof* in Zenettistrasse, in the evenings home to Munich's rock scene. The renovated *Schlachthof* presents top-class music and political cabaret, and has reasonably good food.

There are also several Mediterranean and South American restaurants and some flashy bars. Looks like the Schlachthof Quarter could be going the same way as Schwabing and Haidhausen before it.

Schwabing (right of Leopoldstrasse) [114 C4–5]

This once charming artists' quarter is now given over to the glitzy world of sex shops, cheap pizzerias, Pils bars and billiard halls. Only the street names remind you of the spirit of Schwabing of old: Occam, Wedekind, Werneck. Around Wedekindplatz especially, the gastronomic scene caters largely for passing custom. Here and there, though, you'll find a few little *Insider ip* gems, such as the *Podium*, a smoky music bar featuring Dixieland and rock oldies. In the daytime, a leisurely walk can reveal many examples of the classic architecture of the men of means who settled here following the incorporation of 'Schwapinga' into Greater Munich in 1890.

Schwabing (left of Leopoldstrasse) [114 B4–5] *Insider Tip*

What a difference! The district to the left of Leopoldstrasse is populated by doctors, journalists and artists living in old, large, often expensively renovated apartments with stucco work and huge, Art-Nouveau windows. No end of boutiques and second-hand bookshops alternate with goldsmiths and jewellers. A place to window-shop for hours at a time, buy fresh fruit and vegetables or savour a few oysters at the Elisabeth Market, rummage around in the second-hand shops or one of the countless junk shops. The atmosphere is characterised by the students who play chess in the cafés or soak up Kant's *Critique of Pure Reason* over a swift beer at *Atzinger* (Schellingstrasse). An invisible boundary separates Schwabing from the so-called 'Maxvorstadt', home of the Pinakothek galleries and where students of the Music Academy cycle around, their instruments strapped to their backs. A whiff of old Schwabing is still in the air; the Schwabing of the city executioner, of Wedekind and Ringelnatz, imbued with the spirit which inspired Thomas Mann to write his since much miss-used phrase 'Munich shone', in his novella *Gladius Dei* of 1902.

Sendling [117 D6]

A working-class district which has evolved to the north of the abattoir. It stretches up the Sendlinger Hill, hence the division into Upper and Lower Sendling, the latter being the more attractive part. Here, there are still many beautiful buildings which have not yet been renovated. This too is Munich's Socialist heartland, the ultimate SPD bastion. The Sendlinger Kulturschmiede was the inspiration for similar projects all over the city. Around the wholesale market, numerous restaurants full of Mediterranean flair serve up a multi-cultural feast. It is worth taking a walk down towards the zoo, from Harras to the Brudermühltunnel and through the Flaucher. In summer, it offers an ideal nudist bathing area.

Westend [117 D–E 2–3]

Munich's most colourful and probably most charming district, drenched in the sights, sounds and smells of the Levant: carpet dealers from Istanbul or Antalya display their wares, Turkish names and Arabic signs abound in shop windows. On the menu there's Gyros and Döner Kebab, washed down with the heavy wine from Santorin, Ouzo from Levkas and Raki from Anatolia. This is the home of students and bohemians and beyond the Schwanthaler Höh as far as the central ring road Munich really is a multi-cultural metropolis.

STREETS & SQUARES

Isartorplatz [111 F5]

In the daily rush-hour a catastrophe. This is where the Altstadtring (old town ring road) crosses the main link between Haidhausen and the inner city. Dominated by the Isartor (1337), then the city's eastern gateway and now home to the off-beat Valentin-Karlstadt Musäum, it epitomises Munich's main architectural dilemma: medieval fortifications, post-war eyesores, painstakingly restored houses and ultra-modern blocks clash to make this crazy metropolitan cocktail. *S-Bahn: Isartor*

Karlsplatz (Stachus) [110 B3]

Ticket collectors on the trams still can't decide whether it should be called Karlsplatz or Stachus. Historically speaking, there is no doubt that this square in the heart of the city – laid out in place of the razed city fortifications in 1791 and famed for many years after World War II as the busiest junction in Europe (though not as impressive as London's Piccadilly Circus or the Place de la Concorde in Paris) – was named after the little-loved Elector Karl Theodor. In typical Munich fashion, the name 'Stachus', however, stems probably from the former inn Stachusgarten, which stood where today's Kaufhof department store thrones. To the east, on the right of the neo-Baroque shops and office premises built by architect Gabriel von Seidl, stands the three-arched *Karlstor*, remnant of the 14th-century fortifications and gateway to Neuhauser Strasse and the pedestrian zone. The fountain is a popular meeting place in summer for motorbike tourists. The *Pini-Haus* is typical of the dynamism of the square; until recently home to the city's eco-centre, it has now been turned into a hotel. Where the Stachus meets Lenbachplatz to the north, stands the gleaming white Palace of Justice. Built in the 19th century by architect Friedrich von Thiersch (1852–1921), it is an architectural tribute to Gothic, Renaissance and Baroque culture. *S- and U-Bahn: Stachus*

Karlsplatz, better known as Stachus, is a favourite meeting place

Lenbachplatz [110 B2–3]

Built around the turn of the 20th century and typical of the then upbeat mood in urban planning, unhindered by ideology. The 'Künstlerhaus' (Artists' House) by Gabriel von Seidl has long since lost its importance as an artists' society. Diagonally opposite is the former Bernheim Palace, just one victim of the biggest property scandal in German history, when mogul Jürgen Schneider went bankrupt in 1994. It was renovated at great cost and kitted out with a super-elegant restaurant. *S- and U-Bahn: Stachus*

Leopoldstrasse [114 C1–5]

Opinions differ when it comes to this street, which begins at the Victory Gate and runs way out beyond the Petuel ring road. Hardly a single tourist fails to take an evening stroll from the Siegestor to Münchner Freiheit, starting on the eastern side where hordes of street traders sell artefacts – or so they claim. Countless small cafés and restaurants line the boulevard, the tables of the ice-cream parlours spill out onto the pavement. Boutiques, book shops, record dealers, discos, fast-food and speciality restaurants abound. At the northern end are two small, but famous cinemas, the Leopold in the 'Yellow House' on the corner of Franzstrasse, and the ABC at the junction with Herzogstrasse. To the south, Jonothan Borowsky's *Walking Man* strides out in front of Munich's biggest re-insurance company. Architecturally nothing to write home about, the tourists' favourite Munich street has probably for this reason slid a little down-market, a glittering avenue where you are unlikely to get ripped off, but where nothing comes cheap. The few

Bavarian restaurants are so over-the-top, it'll make your *Weisswurst* burst! *U-Bahn: 3/6, Giselastrasse or Münchner Freiheit*

Ludwigstrasse [118 C1]

A walk down this monumental avenue, from the Field Marshall's Hall in the south, past noble Käfer's restaurant on the Hofgarten towards the City Library and university as far as the Triumphal Arch, will give you a taste of architect Klenze's vision of giving Munich an opulent, homogeneous boulevard as a convincing demonstration of the grandeur of the Bavarian kingdom. *U-Bahn: 3/6, Odeonsplatz or Universitä.*

Marienplatz [111 D4]

Munich's social, economic and architectural heart since it's earliest days. The old 'Schrannenplatz' was lined with market halls and stands, later trams rattled their way across this busy intersection, and since the Olympic building boom it has been a pedestrian zone. The Mariensäule (St Mary's Column) was erected in 1638, the fulfilment of a vow taken by devout Elector Maximilian I, should Munich and Landshut survive intact the Swedish campaign during the Thirty Years' War. With this bronze statue by Hubert Gerhard, the prince further encouraged the cult of the Virgin Mary which was developing at the time in Bavaria. Today, the Marienplatz is not only a must on every tourist sightseeing plan – especially because of the 11 o'clock Glocken-spiel ritual at the New Town Hall – but is also the destination of almost every political demonstration and venue for all manner of municipal

Insider Tip

culture events. Street musicians, jugglers and mimes have made Marienplatz – and Neuhauser Strasse – their own personal, officially sanctioned arena, and are doing very nicely thank you. Architecturally speaking, though, Marienplatz is a bit of a failure. The extravagant New Town Hall is too overpowering, and the Kaufhof department store rates as the height of architectural bad taste. You get a fine view of the hustle and bustle below from the pseudo-noble Metropolitan café, or the aptly named Café Glockenspiel next door (both opposite the New Town Hall). *S- and U-Bahn: Marienplatz*

Maximilianstrasse [111 E–F3]

Munich's showcase avenue also reveals much about the conflicting nature of the city. Just one and a half kilometres long, it rates as one of the great boulevards. It begins, looking eastwards, highly symbolically: at right angles to the (pedestrianised) Residenzstrasse, it radiates out towards the rising sun. On the left, it is flanked by the austere façade of the National Theatre, on the left, at the corner with the Hofgraben, by the Bavarian State Mint, emblazoned with the words 'Moneta Regia', which the locals freely translate as 'Cash rules!'. From 1853 onwards, Maximilian II, disgusted by his father's love of rigid neo-classicism, realised his vision of a more liberal architecture. Court architect Friedrich Bürklein set about mixing Tudor Gothic and Italian late Renaissance elements and French arcades to make a daring architectural cocktail. A century later, the people of Munich managed to wrest this royal concept from the

Exclusive, expensive, elegant: Munich's magnificent Maximilianstrasse

rubble of World War II: standing in the morning facing the sun, you will see beyond the Isar the Classicist seat of the State Parliament, the Maximilianeum, an almost utopian vision. In between, lie Munich's most expensive fashion boutiques, plus a few, tucked-away high-class jewellers, hairdressers and classy bistros. Not to mention the noble Kempinski Vier Jahreszeiten Hotel, the highly praised Kammerspiele theatre and Munich's best-known insider bar, Schumann's. Unfortunately, the central ring road severs this harmonious parade of buildings rather cruelly. The administration of Upper Bavaria sits opposite the monument to Maximilian II, which proudly and defiantly personifies the ideology of the day: justice, military strength, peace and science. Almost every procession leads from the Maximilianeum down the av-

enue into the centre. *U-Bahn: 3/6, Marienplatz or 4/5, Lehel; tram: 19*

Münchner Freiheit [114 C4]
The former Feilitzschplatz was renamed after World War II as a token of remembrance to those who died in the course of their resistance activities against Hitler. In the 1970s, extensive rebuilding work changed the face of the square considerably.

The Münchner Freiheit is many things: traffic intersection, Schwabing's nerve centre, café stronghold and, especially at night, a rowdy entertainment hot spot. Above all, it is symptomatic of Munich life: bustling, showy, frayed at the edges, but also endearing, original, colourful and occasionally cosy – depending on the time of day and your own personal philosophy. *U-Bahn: 3/6, Münchner Freiheit*

I came, I saw, I was impressed!

Munich's museums cover the whole artistic spectrum

Leaving Berlin aside, Munich with almost 50 state, municipal and private collections is the record-holder among the German cities. Its reputation as a museums centre, however, rests above all on its glorious past. It was Bavaria's art-loving King Ludwig I who founded the Alte and Neue Pinakothek, the Glyptothek and the Antikensammlung (State Antiquities Collection) and in so doing made Munich's cultural inheritance accessible to the public. Ludwig's museums are crowd-pullers to this day and constantly set new attendance figure records.

Modern art has long been neglected by comparison. Until 2000, there was no museum dedicated to contemporary art in the Bavarian capital. The Staatsgalerie Moderner Kunst, temporarily located in a side wing of the Haus der Kunst, was bursting at the seams and only able to display a third of its stock from the 20th century. It was left to private collectors and art patrons to fill this gap. Now, however, a new gallery has opened close to the Alte and Neue Pinakotheken. Following the American example, the Pinako-

Whether da Vinci or Dürer – you'll find them in the Alte Pinakothek

thek der Moderne unites not only paintings and sculptures from the Staatsgalerie Moderner Kunst, but also the plentiful stock of arts and crafts and design exhibits from the Neue Sammlung (State Museum of Applied Art).

The most important museums in Munich are situated around the Königsplatz (Glyptothek, State Antiquities Collection, Alte und Neue Pinakothek and Lenbachhaus) and also in the vicinity of Prinzregentenstrasse. Here, conveniently lined up for the visitor, are the Haus der Kunst, the Bayerisches Nationalmuseum, the State Museum of Applied Art and the Schack Gallery; a short walk away are the Prähistorische Staatssammlung (Prehistoric Collection), the Völkerkundemuseum (Ethnological Museum), the Resi-

A superlative work of art in its own right: the Glyptothek

denz, the Ägyptisches Museum (Egyptian Museum) and the Deutsches Museum.

Those visitors who are not drawn to such high-brow establishments, are advised to take a look at the Valentin-Karlstadt-Musäum or one of the many small museums which cater for more exotic interests.

Munich's museums are generally closed on Mondays and public holidays. Admission costs between one and four Euro. On Sundays and public holidays, state-owned museums and the Munich City Museum can be visited free of charge. Schoolchildren, students and senior citizens pay reduced admission charges. Display captions are generally in German, though most galleries have explanatory leaflets or books in English which you can borrow or buy, and some larger museums have taped, self-guided audio tours.

Alpines Museum   **[119 D3]**
The Alpine Museum has a permanent collection on mountaineering and topical, temporary displays, plus an archive packed with information on all things alpine. *Tues to Fri 1 pm–6 pm, Sat&Sun 11 am–6 pm; Praterinsel 5; U-Bahn: 4/5, Lehel*

Alte Pinakothek   **[114 B6]**
★ After years of restoration work, the interior of the museum shines in all its former glory. The Alte Pinakothek, the 'old art gallery', contains some 1,400 old masters. Admittedly you won't find Leonardo da Vinci's *Mona Lisa*, but his *Virgin and Child with a Vase of Flowers,* and Lorenzo Lotto's *Mystic marriage of St Catherine*. The Alte Pinakothek is one of the six most important art galleries in the world. Its collection of paintings represents all European schools from the Middle Ages to the beginning of the 19th century, concentrating in particular on German and Dutch paintings of the 15th and 16th centuries, 17th-century Dutch and Flemish art, Italian paintings from the 15th to 18th centuries as well as French and Spanish Baroque painting.

The most prized treasure is Albrecht Dürer's *Four Apostles* dating back to 1526, which was brought, in return for political aid, from Nuremberg to Munich. Well worth seeing are also the old German masters ranging from Altdorfer to Cranach on the upper floor, the 15th- and 16th-century Italians, the Rubens Gallery, the French works of the 17th century, Tiepolo's *Adoration of the Kings* and Jan Brueghel the Elder's *Fish Market* from 1603. Lovers of Swabian painting will find on the ground floor the wings of the altar from the Cistercian Abbey Church at Kaisheim, painted by Hans Holbein the Elder.

Leo von Klenze, King Ludwig I's famous court master builder, incorporated several architectural innovations in the Alte Pinakothek. Not only did he install the first visible overhead windows in a museum, but also introduced a completely new layout plan which was dictated by the type of available light and its angle of incidence. Klenze's 19th-century building, oriented towards the Italian Renaissance style, was to exert an influence on museum building techniques all over Europe. *Daily, except Mon 10 am–5 pm, Thurs 10 am–8 pm; www.pinakotheken-muenchen.de;*

MARCO POLO **Highlights** »Museums«

★ **Alte Pinakothek**
Artistic masterpieces housed in an architectural masterpiece (page 40)

★ **Pinakothek der Moderne**
New home for new art (page 46)

★ **Deutsches Museum**
What, why, and how? Life's burning questions on science and technology (page 42)

★ **Münchner Stadtmuseum**
An historical potpourri, masterfully united under one roof (page 44)

★ **Valentin-Karlstadt-Musäum**
Have an open mind for German humour (page 47)

★ **Glyptothek**
For classicists and other connoisseurs (page 43)

★ **Haus der Kunst**
For fans of international art and bombastic Nazi architecture (page 43)

★ **Neue Pinakothek**
For art lovers with time to spare (page 45)

★ **Lenbachhaus**
Modern art in old framework (page 44)

★ **Villa Stuck**
Highly individual work by 'prince of painters' Franz von Stuck (page 47)

Barerstrasse 27; U-Bahn: 2, Königsplatz; tram: 27

Insider Tip
Bayerisches Nationalmuseum   [119 D2]

Those of you who are interested in Bavarian and Southern German art and civilisation cannot afford to miss the National Museum in Prinzregentenstrasse. It is several museums rolled into one: Western art history (especially sculpture, from the early Middle Ages to the mid-19th century); arts and crafts (porcelain, ceramics, gem cutting, gold and silverwork, glass painting, clocks, miniatures, etc.); civilisation (folk art, religious folk art, crib collection). Of particular interest are the sculptures by Tilmann Leinberger, pictures by Grasser and Polack, the Ignaz Günther Room, the Landshut and Schwanthal Rooms, the Tattenbach Collection and the Augsburg weaving workshop on the ground floor. In addition, there is a comprehensive collection of Meissen and Nymphenburg porcelain, plus farmhouse parlours, masks and potters' tools. The crib collection features more than 6,000 figures and is unrivalled anywhere in the world – a popular attraction, not just around Christmas. *Apr to Sept: daily, except Mon 10 am to 5 pm, Thurs 10 am–8 pm; Oct–Mar: daily, except Mon 9 am–4 pm; Sun and public hols: free admission; Prinzregentenstrasse 3; U-Bahn: 4/5, Lehel; bus: 53; tram: 17*

BMW-Museum
Zeithorizont [114 A2]

The museum, a giant, windowless reinforced concrete bowl, stands directly alongside the BMW headquarters. From the legendary prewar 'Dixi', via the Isetta to the extravagant sports and racing cars of the 1950s and 1960s, from the BMW R 32, the first motorbike with transverse Boxer engine and triangular frame, to the world-record-breaking machine of 1955 – just about everything which the Bayerischen Motorenwerke have put on the market is here. *Daily 9 am–5 pm (last admission: 4 pm); Petuelring 130; U-Bahn: 3, Olympiazentrum*

Deutsches Jagd-
und Fischereimuseum [110 B3]

El Dorado for fans of huntin', shootin' and fishin' from all corners of the globe. Some 500 preserved life-size specimens of wild animals, displayed in dioramas representing their natural habitats. Add to this a magnificent collection of weapons and hunting equipment from several centuries, exhibits on falconry, palaeontological skeletons (giant Irish stag), trophies, plus fish and angling equipment (fishing tackle from the Stone Age to the present day). There are special hands-on sections for children and also for blind visitors. Just for a laugh, there's also a collection of 'Wolpertingers', a mythical animal of Bavarian legend! *Daily 9.30 am to 5 pm; in winter: until 4 pm; Mon& Thurs 9.30 am–9 pm; Neuhauser Strasse 2; S- and U-Bahn: Stachus*

Deutsches Museum [118 C3–4]

★ Three weeks would probably not be sufficient to do justice to the Deutsches Museum. With 55,000 sq m of exhibition space and

Deutsches Museum: aviation department at Schleissheim

around 17,000 exhibits, it is one of the largest science and technology museums in the world. The collection, begun in 1903 by Oskar von Miller, is constantly being added to and complemented with the latest technological developments, for example the brand-new chronology department. This mega-show on the island in the middle of the Isar covers just about every technical invention known to man.

Visitors must be prepared to leave a lot out, though. The main attractions include the replica mine in the basement, the aviation and maritime galleries, the automobile and railway departments and the huge 'Faraday Cage' in the electrical power section *(demonstrations: daily 11 am, 2 pm and 4 pm)*. Take time to visit the Zeiss Planetarium in the newly opened 'Forum der Technik' (Technical Forum) *(demonstrations: 10 am, noon, 2 pm and 4 pm). Daily 9 am–5 pm; reduced admission for groups of 20 and over; www.Deutsches-Museum. de; Museumsinsel 1; S-Bahn: Isartor; tram: 18.*

The Deutsches Museum opened a separate aviation department at Schleissheim in 1992. *Daily 9 am–5 pm (except national public holidays); Effnerstrasse 18, Oberschleissheim; S-Bahn: 1 (direction: Freising), Oberschleissheim*

Glyptothek [118 A1]

★ Munich's oldest museum and at the same time one of the first public museums in Europe. The Glyptothek on Königsplatz, King Ludwig I's famous antiquities collection, opened its doors in 1830, predating even the British Museum in London or the Hermitage in St Pe-

tersburg. A perfect synthesis of form and content: one of Europe's most spectacular sculpture collections housed in one of Germany's most important Classicist buildings. Most of the works on display are, however, copies.

Designed by Leo von Klenze (1784–1864) in the style of an Ionic temple, the museum contains Greek and Roman sculptures dating from the 6th century BC to the 4th century AD. It is worth taking a look at all 13 exhibition rooms, concentrating perhaps on a few individual pieces. The Barberini Faun in erotic pose appears surprisingly modern; hard to believe he's over 2,000 years old (Room II). The 62 Roman busts on limestone pillars (of varying heights to indicate the status of the portrayed person) are particularly impressive (Room XI). The most precious items are the well-preserved original statues from of the Aphaia Temple on the island of Aegina (500 BC) (Rooms VII and IX).

The inner courtyard of the Glyptothek is an idyllic refuge from Munich's hectic streets: a café beneath acacia trees and between the vine-clad museum walls inspires you to be creative yourself or just dream a little. *Wed, Fri, Sat, Sun 10 am–5 pm, Tues&Thurs 10 am–8 pm; Sun: free admission; Königsplatz 3; U-Bahn: 2, Königsplatz*

Haus der Kunst [118 C1]

★ A prime example of bombastic Nazi architecture. The east wing of the 'House of Art' is used to stage temporary exhibitions, while the west wing is now home to the Theater im Haus der Kunst and the Bayerisches Staatsschauspiel. In

September 2002, the Staatsgalerie Moderner Kunst (Modern Art Gallery), which had been temporarily housed in the west wing, moved to the brand new Pinakothek der Moderne. *Daily 10 am–10 pm, Sun and public hols: free admission; Prinzregentenstrasse 1; U-Bahn: 3/ 4/5/6, Odeonsplatz; bus: 53*

Kunsthalle der Hypo-Kulturstiftung   [111 D3]

Fine surroundings for some fine works of art. Changing exhibitions of art from the Renaissance to the present day. Lovingly restored and integrated in the Five Courtyards. *Daily 10 am–8 pm; Theatinerstrasse 8; U-Bahn: 3/6, Marienplatz or Odeonsplatz*

Lenbachhaus   [118 A1]

★ Just a stone's throw from Königsplatz is one of Munich's loveliest museums: the former villa of 'prince of painters', Franz von Lenbach. Stepping through the wrought-iron gateway, you will discover not only an art collection, but also an oasis of peace and relaxation. The works of the Städtische Galerie have been housed in this ochre-coloured, Italian-style villa and artist's residence since 1929. This comprehensive collection documents the history of art in Munich from the Gothic period to the present. The main emphasis, however, is on the 19th century (Lenbach estate) and on the 20th century (Art Nouveau, Paul Klee collection, Kubin Archive).

The museum owes its international reputation to the Blue Rider Collection. In addition to the famous works by Franz Marc, Gabriele Münter, Alexej von

Modelled on a Renaissance Italian country villa: the Lenbachhaus

Jawlenksy, August Macke and Paul Klee, we recommend you pay particular attention to the broad selection of paintings by Wassily Kandinsky, donated to the museum in 1957 by his partner of many years, Gabriele Münter. The ground floor shows temporary exhibitions of contemporary art. Lectures, concerts and film and video presentations complete the picture. *Daily, except Mon 10 am–6 pm; Luisenstrasse 33 (at the corner of Briennerstrasse); U-Bahn: 2, Königsplatz*

Münchner Stadtmuseum   [111 D5]

★ Munich City Museum on St-Jakobs-Platz is not a local-history museum in the true sense of the word. The core of the exhibition was originally a large collection of historical weapons, small sculptures (Morris Dancers), coins and medals, folk objects and textiles (bridal accessories, traditional costumes, cribs). Among the interesting specialist museums in the building are a large puppet theatre department (with over 50,000 puppets) and a sizeable collection of musical instruments. There is also a Fashion Museum (with clothing, accessories, prints and photographs from the 18th century to the present), plus a Film and Photography Museum (two public screenings per day in the museum cinema). Don't miss the original temporary exhibitions in the City Museum on such themes as 'Death', 'The Loo', or 'Oktoberfest'. *Tues–Sun 10 am–6 pm; St-Jakobs-Platz 1; S- and U-Bahn: Marienplatz*

Museum Mensch und Natur [112 A4]

The Museum of Man and Nature provides an impressive insight into our planet. The colourful world of minerals plus the history of life on Earth are vividly illustrated and explained – a must not only for children. *Closed until mid-2003 for renovation; Maria-Ward-Strasse 16; bus: 41; tram: 17*

Neue Pinakothek [118 B1]

★ As a counterpart to the Alte Pinakothek directly opposite, Ludwig I founded the Neue Pinakothek in the mid-19th century. It was the first museum for contemporary art in Europe to open its doors to the general public. Irreparably damaged in World War II, the old Klenze building had to be demolished, and was replaced by Alexander von Branca's new gallery. Opened in 1981, the largest newly-built post-

Unusual Museums

Comical collections for all five senses

ZAM is the abbreviation for 'Zentrum für außergewöhnliche Museen' (Centre for Unusual Museums). A treasure trove for fans of those phenomena of cultural history which are otherwise simply overlooked or deliberately side-lined. As you can imagine, there's a Perfume Museum (Patrick Süskind, author of *Perfume*, was born here after all). This splendid institution also brings together, among other things, museums dedicated to chamber pots, pedal cars, so-called *bourdalou* (exquisitely decorated portable toilets for 18th- and 19th-century ladies) and locks (including a wooden ruff collar worn as a punishment by naughty girls in the 17th century!). Unfortunately for visitors, they are not permitted to try out the exhibits in any of the museums! This wise precaution also applies of course at the Easter Bunny Museum – otherwise, there would soon be no exhibits left! *Daily 10 am–6 pm; Westenriederstrasse 41* [111 E5]; *S-Bahn: Isartor*

war museum in Germany was greeted with much enthusiasm, but also critical discussion.

Interest in the new building is unbroken. Its one millionth visitor passed through the doors just one year after the official opening. The 22 exhibition rooms, arranged on varying levels, contain some 550 paintings and 50 sculptures from the time between the Rococo and Art-Nouveau periods – these represent only around a tenth of the total collection. Backbone of the collection is European art of the 19th century. The concept behind the individual rooms aims to highlight the great variety of 19th-century art schools and compare and contrast their styles, ranging from the early Romantics, courtly art under Ludwig I, the Nazarenes, French and German late Romantics and Realists to the 'Deutschrömer' (von Marées, Böcklin, Feuerbach), the paintings of the 'Gründerzeit' and the French Impressionists (Degas, Manet, Monet, Renoir). If 19th-century art is not to your taste, you should turn your attention to the early modern age: Impressionists, Secessionists, Symbolists and Art Nouveau (Rooms 18–22). Special exhibitions in the basement. *Wed and Fri–Mon 10 am–5 pm, Thurs 10 am–10 pm, Sun and public hols: free admission; www.pinakotheken-muenchen.de; Barerstrasse 29 (northern entrance); U-Bahn: 2, Theresienstrasse; tram: 18*

Pinakothek der Moderne [118 B1]

★ The Pinakothek der Moderne, opened in September 2002, is the latest component in the ensemble loosely termed the 'Kunstareal München'. Within short walking distances of one another, the Pinakothek galleries, the sculpture and antiquities collections and the

Café at the Neue Pinakothek: after 22 rooms, take a well-earned break

Lenbachhaus are now joined by a stunning work of art in itself, which brings the Munich museum landscape right into the 21st century. The opening of this new box of treasures means a kind of 'coming home' for several collections which have hitherto only been shown in temporary settings and on a reduced scale.

Four major collections belonging to the Free State, plus a series of valuable private donations are united under one roof. Alongside design, graphic art and architecture, the Staatsgalerie Moderner Kunst (State Gallery for Modern Art) has finally found a permanent home. The collection features paintings and sculptures of the 20th century, beginning with the German Expressionists right down to the American minimalists of the 1970s and contemporary Italian art. Overall, some 500 exhibits are on display in around 5,500 sq m of exhibition rooms. Curator Carla Schulz-Hoffmann has managed to highlight the common elements which characterise artistic development in the 20th century, without jeopardising the individuality of each discipline. Special events will also emphasise the interrelationship between visual and non-visual art forms. *Tues&Wed and Sat&Sun 10 am–5 pm, Thurs& Fri 10 am–8 pm; www.pinakothek-der-moderne.de; Barerstrasse 40; U-Bahn: 2, Theresienstrasse*

Valentin-Karlstadt-Musäum [111 F5]

★ The Isartor is home to one of Munich's most popular and amusing museums, dedicated to one of Germany's favourite comic actors, Karl Valentin (1882–1967). Although his humour can be difficult to appreciate for non-German-speakers, his visual, slapstick style has a universal appeal. At the top of the tower there is a café, furnished in the typical coffee house style of the turn of the 19th century, with its own resident musician. Incidentally, persons over 99 years of age get in free if accompanied by their parents! *Mon, Tues, Fri, Sat 11.01 am–17.29 pm, Sun 10.01 am–17.29 pm; Tal 43; S-Bahn: Isartor*

Insider Tip

Villa Stuck [119 E2]

★ In the middle of Munich's classy Bogenhausen district, behind the Friedensengel (Angel of Peace) atop its column, stands the neo-Classicist palace of that other 'prince of painters' Franz von Stuck. Von Stuck himself designed both exterior and interior of this highly individual, giant work of art. Completed in 1898, the artist's villa was the glittering focal point of city society during his lifetime. Visit the prestigious salons on the ground floor, with their magnificent wall decorations and display of von Stuck's paintings, sculptures and extravagant furniture. Upstairs, the atelier features a splendid coffered ceiling. Here, too, hang several beautiful Gobelin tapestries – if the walls are not hung with other works of art at the time. Excellent temporary exhibitions of art of the turn of the century and the Art-Nouveau era. Note also the bronze statue of the amazon on horseback in the garden in front of the villa's colonnaded doorway, von Stuck's sculptural masterpiece. *Daily, except Mon 10 am–6 pm; Prinzregentenstrasse 60; U-Bahn: 4, Prinzregentenplatz; bus: 53; tram: 18*

Beer gardens, bistros and gourmet temples

Munich dishes up not only beer and Weisswurst; it caters equally well for the refined palate, too

The diverse charms of regional cuisine are experiencing a revival, even in top-class restaurants. Bavarian cooking is by no means just *Leberkäs* (meatloaf) and *Weisswurst* (veal sausage), *Schweinsbraten* (pork roast) and *Knödel* (dumplings), though these are delicious in their own right. Bavarian cooking – and that of its capital – is more varied, sophisticated and actually more individual than you might expect. The choice is yours.

As in all major cities in recent years, Munich has seen the establishment of many French, Asian and Italian restaurants. There are numerous bistros and snack bars serving tasty specialities from countries with a tradition of fine cooking. Yet local delicacies are not neglected either, such as *Kalbsbries* (sweetbread of calf) and *Saure Lüngerl* (pickled lung). Meat is a traditional staple in Bavaria, and despite the dangers of BSE, gout and increased levels of heavy metals, animal innards are particularly

Break beneath palms and glass cupola: Café Luitpold

Whether Italian espresso or Japanese sushi, cool surroundings are in

popular. *Kalbshirn* (calves' brain, fried in breadcrumbs) can be delicious; pigs and calves' kidneys are served either sour (with vinegar) or fried; calves' lung cooked slowly is then served with dumplings.

Take fish: thanks to the cleanness of Bavarian lakes (Chiemsee water has once again attained the quality of drinking water), supplies are plentiful, though perhaps not very varied. Try the famous white-fish from Lake Starnberg, or some trout – though more likely to come from a farm than a mountain stream, it's on every menu.

Here are a few tips when reading the menu. If it says 'Schweinebraten' and not 'Schweinsbraten', then things are not as Bavarian as they might seem. If the beer is served in 0.33-litre glasses, the North German influence has got the upper hand. Where 'Kalbsmedaillon und Pommes de terre' (médaillons of veal with potatoes) is on the menu, you'll be paying a lot of money for something untypical of Munich.

Munich's waiters and waitresses, at least in the 'genuine' traditional inns, are often a little on the grumpy side. Going Dutch when paying the bill is no problem, and it is customary to add up to ten per cent as a tip, or at least round up the amount charged. Guests tend to leave the table fairly soon after finishing their meal. Don't hesitate to have a well-earned compliment passed on to the chef – it will increase your chances of being served more courteously the next time!

BEER GARDENS

Almost all beer gardens close at 10 pm. If not otherwise specified, they open daily.

Augustinerkeller [117 E1]

Inside Tip

Legendary *Stammtisch* (table reserved for regulars). A veritable shrine to traditional beer garden culture, serving a superb freshly tapped beer. *Arnulfstrasse 52; Tel. 59 43 93; S- and U-Bahn: Hauptbahnhof*

Aumeister [115 F1]

Inside Tip

🏃 At the northern end of the English Garden, unfortunately too close to the Bavarian Broadcasting Corporation studios. Pleasant in hot summers, thanks to the fine trees. *Daily, except Mon, from 9 am; Sondermeierstrasse 1; Tel. 32 52 24; U-Bahn: 6, Freimann*

Beer garden idyll on the Kleinhesseloher See in the Englischer Garten

MARCO POLO **Highlights** »Food & Drink«

★ **Aroma Kaffeebar**
As cosy as your own kitchen – but the cake here tastes better (page 53)

★ **Geisel's Vinothek**
400 delicious wines to taste and to buy (page 57)

★ **Gasthaus Glockenbach**
German cooking with a noble touch (page 56)

★ **Makassar**
Mediterranean and Creole (page 57)

★ **Franziskaner Fuchsenstubn**
The finest Weisswurst for Munich's political elite (page 59)

★ **Weisses Bräuhaus**
Typical: good food and a warm welcome (page 61)

★ **Il Soprano**
A secret we'd rather keep to ourselves (page 60)

★ **Andechser am Dom**
No need to say grace! (page 56)

★ **Blaues Haus**
Finest Bavarian cooking, with a hint of the South and a cast of theatrical regulars (page 59)

★ **Fraunhofer**
Munich's oldest student pub (page 59)

Chinesischer Turm [115 D6]
🏃 Constructed in 1789, the Chinese Tower is the focal point of the city's most famous beer garden. Meeting place of the punk and the prominent. Be warned: there's 'oompah music' on Sundays, your glass might not be as full as it should be and it's generally very crowded. *Englischer Garten 3; Tel. 383 87 30; U-Bahn: 3/6, Giselastrasse; bus: 54*

Flaucher [0]
Good, solid fare in the open, close to the sun-worshippers on the Flaucher beaches. Ideal after a trip to the zoo. *Daily, except Mon, from 10 am (depending on the weather); Isarauen 1; Tel. 723 26 77; U-Bahn: 3, Thalkirchen*

Wirtshaus im Grüntal [115 F4]
You can tell by the cars parked outside, this is a spot for 'beautiful people'. *Daily 11 am–11 pm; Grüntal 15; Tel. 998 41 10; bus: 87*

Königlicher Hirschgarten [112 B6] *Insider Tip*
Biggest, finest, friendliest Munich beer garden – and long may it stay that way! So please, don't tell your friends! *Daily 9 am–midnight; Hirschgartenallee 1; Tel. 17 25 91; S-Bahn: Laim; bus: 41, 68; tram: 17, Steubenplatz*

Iberl [0]
Situated in up-market Solln, with guests and prices to match. Inside, lively dialect theatre. *Daily 4 pm to midnight; Wilhelm-Leibl-Strasse*

Gourmet Restaurants in Munich

Bistro restaurant in the Kempinski Vier Jahreszeiten [111 F3]

Still run on traditional Walterspiel lines. The height of eating pleasure at prices to match. Tip: business lunch for 29 Euro. *Daily 6.30 am to 11 am (breakfast), noon–3 pm (lunch), 6 pm–11.30 pm (dinner); Maximilianstrasse 17; Tel. 212 50; U-Bahn: 4/5, Lehel*

Käfer-Schänke [119 E2]

Haven for expense-account plunderers and, with all due respect for some of the dishes, most typical of what the new Munich culinary scene has to offer. À la carte soup from 8 Euro, main course from 19 Euro. *Mon–Sat 11.30 am–1 am; Prinzregentenstrasse 73; Tel. 416 82 47; U-Bahn: 4, Prinzregentenplatz*

Königshof [110 B3]

Enjoy prize-winning cuisine (one star), a pleasant, refined atmosphere, fantastic service and, from your seat by the window, a view of the Stachus. Evening menu around 75 Euro. *Tues–Sat 6.30 am to 10.30 am, noon–3 pm, 6.45 pm to 1 am; Karlsplatz 25; Tel. 55 13 60; S- and U-Bahn: Stachus*

landersdorfer & innerhofer [110 C4]

Latest candidate for a star and any number of other awards. In the heart of the city, an Austro-Bavarian culinary revolution: traditional standards re-interpreted. Especially recommendable at lunchtime: there's no set menu, the waiter reels off the dishes of the day (soup plus main course: 15 Euro). *Mon–Fri 11.30 am–2 pm, 6.30 pm–1 am; Hackenstrasse 6–8; Tel. 26 01 86 37; S- and U-Bahn: Marienplatz*

Restaurant am Marstall [111 F3]

This star-rated newcomer on the gastronomic scene may not be particularly cosy, but all the more innovative in cooking terms. You could easily run up a 75-Euro bill – per head. *Tues–Sat noon–2 pm, 6 pm–10 pm; Maximilianstrasse 16; Tel. 29 16 55 11; S- and U-Bahn: Marienplatz*

Tantris [115 D3]

Munich's longest-serving star-encrusted temple. Masterful *Nouvelle Cuisine* which is not so much new as well-established. Lunch menu from 58 Euro, evening menu from 105 Euro. *Tues–Sat noon–3 pm, 6.30 pm–1 am; Johann-Fichte-Strasse 7; Tel. 361 95 90; U-Bahn: 6, Dietlindenstrasse*

Vinaiolo [119 D4]

Crowned with a star in 1999, chef Andrea Bressan stage-manages his Italian creations right down to the last bite. The selection of wines is enormous – enough to surprise many a connoisseur. Menu approx. 40 Euro. *Tues–Sun noon–3 pm, 6.30 pm–1 am, Mon 6.30 pm–1 am; Steinstrasse 42; Tel. 48 95 03 56; S-Bahn: Rosenheimer Platz*

22; Tel. 79 42 14; S-Bahn: 7, Solln; bus: 66

Taxisgarten [113 D4]

🏃 Bavarian beer garden with student touch. Fresh pretzels every hour. Mostly overcrowded. *Taxisstrasse 12; Tel. 15 68 27; U-Bahn: 1, Gern; bus: 177*

Waldwirtschaft [0]

🏃 Famous for triggering the 1995 'Beer Garden Revolution', to the annoyance of the neighbours who protested against the Dixieland music and to the delight of the guests who love the music and are still prepared to pay the up-market prices in this up-market district. *Mon–Sat 11 am–11 pm; Grosshesselohe, Georg-Kalb-Strasse 3; Tel. 74 99 40 30; S-Bahn: 7, Grosshesselohe*

CAFÉS

Aroma Kaffebar [110 B1]

★ It's small and cramped, and the stools along the right-hand bar leave you staring at the wall. That said, this mini-café is the epitome of Glockenbach charm, and sells cakes with such fabulous names as 'Liza Minnelli's Apricot Stage with Heart-Warming Apricot Liqueur' (2.50 Euro). *Tues–Fri 7 am–6.30 pm, Sat 9 am–4 pm; Pestalozzistrasse 24; U-Bahn: 1/2/3/6, Sendlinger Tor*

Café am Beethovenplatz [117 F3]

How about Chopin and chocolate gateau or Mozart and Mozzarella? The food is good and the temptation is to drink too much. Friendly student-style service. Live jazz for breakfast on Sundays! *Daily 9 am to 1 am; Goethestrasse 51; U-Bahn: 3/6, Goetheplatz*

Café Freiheit [113 D5]

Neon lights, glass-topped tables and a curved bar from the days of the kidney-shaped table all go to make this supposedly the ultimate Yuppie café in town. Good food in the evenings. *Daily 9 am–1 am; Leonrodstrasse/Landshuter Allee; U-Bahn: 1, Rotkreuzplatz*

Friesische Teestube [114 B4] *Insider Tip*

Small, but cosy and plush like grandma's sitting room. More than 150 (!) types of tea and an excellent, inexpensive breakfast. The author's favourite pre-lunch haunt. *Daily 10 am–11 pm; Pündterplatz 2; U-Bahn: 6, Münchner Freiheit; bus: 33, Herzogstrasse*

Café Glockenspiel [111 D4]

Scene meeting place with the best view of Marienplatz and the New

*See and be seen:
café on Maximilianstrasse*

Munich Specialities

Tuck into these delicacies!

Aufgschmalzene Brotsuppe – once a poor man's meal, nowadays on every up-market regional menu. Scraps of bread are soaked overnight in stock; onions, carrots, celeriac, leek and parsley are roasted in dripping and then served in the soup. Served with sausage made from pancreas sweetbread.

Böfflamot – like so much in Bavaria, this derives from the French, namely *bœuf à la mode*. Ox meat is braised together with two calves' feet for four hours.

Leberkäs – a slice in a bread roll is the No.1 survival tactic for lunchers in a hurry. It contains neither liver nor cheese – although the name leads you to expect these – but is a secret combination of beef, pork and other ingredients.

Obatzda – 'Batzen' means a lump of anything soft. Obatzda is a mature Camembert, mixed with butter, onions, paprika, pepper, salt and a drop of beer to make a smooth, thick paste.

Rindsrouladen mit Rahm-karfiol – beef roulade filled with mangelwurzel, mustard, glazed onions and a little bacon, served with cauliflower in a creamy sauce.

Saure Nieren mit Röstkar-toffeln – Innards are unhealthy, but delicious. The trick is to wash the kidneys thoroughly and soak them for half an hour in milk. Then add a shot of lemon juice. Peel and boil potatoes, slice and fry gently in a pan until golden brown.

Schweinsbraten – Pork roast, seasoned with salt, pepper and ground caraway seeds. Score the rind and add a quartered onion to the roasting tin. Baste with dark wheat beer. Serve with dumplings. Beware: if the menu says 'Schweinebraten' instead of 'Schweinsbraten' – it might not be the real McCoy!

Serviettenkloss – Dumpling dough is wrapped tightly in a serviette and cooked for half an hour in boiling water.

Zwetschgenpavesen – The name of this dessert comes from the Italian *zuppa pavese*. It consists of pureed plums, stale bread rolls, milk, eggs, breadcrumbs, clarified butter, sugar and cinnamon.

Town Hall, plus the craziest drinks. *Daily 10 am–1 am; Marienplatz 28; S- and U-Bahn: Marienplatz*

Café Haidhausen [119 D4]

For that special breakfast, with such promising names as 'Romeo and Juliet'. *Mon–Fri 9 am–1 am, Sat& Sun 10 am–1 am; (breakfast until 4 pm); Franziskanerstrasse 4; Tel. 688 60 43; S-Bahn: Rosenheimer Platz*

Cafe Luitpold [111 E2]

The place to go if you are one of the 'beautiful people' or nostalgic at heart. Palm trees, glass cupola and fine cakes. *Sun–Fri 9 am–8 pm, Sat 8 am–7 pm; Brienner Strasse 11; U-Bahn: 3/4/5/6, Odeonsplatz*

MUC [114 C5]

Although the airport is miles away, the 'Café Munich' transports you to distant lands in slick, American style. Tex-Mex, burritos, crêpes. Happy Hour from 5 pm to 8 pm and Midnight Margaritas at half price make that jailbird's breakfast (dry bread, tap water and a cigarette) taste wonderful. *Sun–Thurs 8 am to 3 am, Fri&Sat 8 am–4 am; Leopoldstrasse 9; U-Bahn: 3/6, Giselastrasse*

Rottenhöfer/Café Hag [111 E3]

Superlative confectionery with café. Where the tasty morsels are worth every penny. *Mon–Fri 8.45 am to 7 pm, Sat 8 am–6 pm; Residenzstrasse 26; U-Bahn: 3/4/5/6, Odeonsplatz*

Sarcletti [113 D5]

The home of the most famous – and best – Italian ice-cream in Munich. Fans queue up outside in summer.

Pavement café outside. *Daily 8 am to 11.30 pm; Nymphenburger Strasse 155; U-Bahn: 1, Rotkreuzplatz*

Stadtcafé [111 C5]

🏃 Despite its waiting-room atmosphere, the place to be for young film-makers, cineastes (film museum on the premises) and journalists, with lovingly chosen, top-quality wines. Also a favourite with visitors to the Munich City Museum. Don't miss the duck parfait – it's a must. *Mon–Thurs 11 am–midnight, Fri&Sat 11 am–1 am, Sun 10.30 am–midnight; St-Jakobs-Platz 1; S- and U-Bahn: Marienplatz*

Caffè Streiflicht [110 C4]

In the *Süddeutsche Zeitung* building, and just as keen to keep its customers. The coffee is excellent, whichever way you drink it, though occasionally the combination of music and TV news leaves you lost for words. The alcoholic drinks are too expensive. *Mon–Fri 8.30 am to 9 pm, Sat 9 am–6 pm; Sendlinger Strasse 8; S- and U-Bahn: Marienplatz*

Café Wiener Platz [119 D3]

🏃 *Zeitgeist* café for magazine reporters, ballet dancers and would-be actors. *Daily 8 am–1 am; Innere Wiener Strasse 48; U-Bahn: 4/5, Max-Weber-Platz*

RESTAURANTS €€€

Bistro Terrine [114 B6]

Located in Schwabing's chic Amalienpassage, bite-sized portions of Nouvelle Cuisine. *Tues–Fri noon–3 pm, 6.30 pm–1 am, Sat&Mon 6.30 pm to 1 am; Amalienstrasse 89; Tel. 28 17 80; U-Bahn: 3/6, Universität*

Die Ente vom Lehel   [119 F1]

The duck is back! Ex-Ente (duck) boss and Pump, Duck & Circumstances chef Hanspeter Wodarz works here in an advisory capacity. In the capable hands of Hans-Peter Pinkowsky, the cuisine has an international flavour, absolutely in keeping with the character of the new Arabella Sheraton Grand Hotel. *Tues–Sat 6 pm–midnight; Arabellastrasse 6; Tel. 92 64 81 10; U-Bahn: 4, Arabellapark*

Gasthaus Glockenbach   [117 F4]

★ Karl Ederer, once top 'young gun' on the Munich culinary scene, is still worth a visit, even if 'young' no longer quite fits. Appearances can be deceptive; unprepossessing exterior, but inside the French-style dishes are superb at this star-rated restaurant in the 'Schlachthof' district. *Tues–Sat noon–3 pm, 7 pm–1 am; Kapuzinerstrasse 29; Tel. 538 97 31; U-Bahn: 3/6, Goetheplatz*

Kleinschmitz   [118 B3]

For the connoisseur who likes food without fuss. French tinge to the cuisine, varied selection of wine, also to take away. *Daily 7 pm–1 am; Fraunhoferstrasse 13; Tel. 260 85 18; U-Bahn:1/2, Fraunhoferstrasse*

Schuhbeck's in den Südtiroler Stuben   [111 E4]

He's found his way into the big city at last: Alfons Schuhbeck, Michelin-star chef from Waging am See, has taken over the former Torrgelstuben, and serves up his interpretation of regional cuisine. *Daily 11.30 am–2.30 pm, 6 pm–10.30 pm; Am Platzl 6 and 8; Tel. 216 69 00; S- and U-Bahn: Marienplatz*

Heavenly delights from Andechs Monastery now in the city centre

RESTAURANTS €€

Andechser am Dom   [111 D3]

★ Praise be to God! The beer-brewing monks from Andechs Monastery have opened a place of culinary pilgrimage in Munich. The spectrum ranges from sausage salad to pikeperch with truffles. No need to say grace, just enjoy Bavaria's best beer! *Daily 10 am–1 am; Weinstrasse 7a; Tel. 29 84 81; S- and U-Bahn: Marienplatz*

Eisbach – Bar & Küche   [111 F3]

A veritable melting pot of world cooking – Asian and American seasoned European-style. Ideal, too, for a snack after the theatre. *Daily 10 am–1 am; Marstallplatz 3; Tel. 22 80 17 81; U-Bahn: 3/6, Odeonsplatz*

Formula 1 Szenario   [114 C5]

Formerly known to Munich experts as the Extrablatt. The new proprietor Umberto Nasuti is a Ferrari freak, though his prices are around BMW level, as is the cooking. *Daily 9 am–2 am; Leopoldstrasse 7; Tel. 33 20 00; U-Bahn: 3/6, Giselastrasse*

FOOD & DRINK

Geisel's Vinothek   [110 A3]
★ Gourmet stronghold close to the station. The chef has been rewarded with a star. In terms of atmosphere, though, the restaurant is in a class of its own. *Daily 11 am–1 am; Schützenstrasse 11; Tel. 55 13 71 40; S- and U-Bahn: Hauptbahnhof*

Il Grappolo   [114 B5]
'In vino veritas' – 'Truth comes out in wine'. Put this Latin allegation to the test not far from the university in one of the nicest Italian restaurants. It's more of a living room for a maximum of 50 people. Almost too good for a city guide. *Mon–Sat 11.30 am–11.30 pm; Adalbertstrasse 28; Tel. 39 62 41; U-Bahn: 3/6, Universität*

Grüne Gans   [111 D5]
Just 25 places at which to enjoy food of the highest quality. New menu every day and vegetables fresh from the market. *Mon–Sat 5 pm–1 am; Am Einlass 5; Tel. 26 62 28; S- and U-Bahn: Marienplatz*

Käfer's am Hofgarten   [111 E2]
Where else could you find *Baby-leberkäs'* on the menu, but at this spin-off from the mega delicatessen? *Sun–Thurs 9 am–1 am, Fri&Sat 9 am–2 am; Odeonsplatz 6–7; Tel. 290 75 30; U-Bahn: 3/6, Odeonsplatz*

Lenbach   [110 B2]
In-crowd eatery. Stefan Marquard cooks the way he looks: wild, extravagant and he isn't afraid to improvise. Pompous and huge, but a real experience. *Mon–Fri 11.30 am–2.30 pm, 6 pm–1 am, Sat 6 pm–1 am; Ottostrasse 6; Tel. 549 13 00; S- and U-Bahn: Stachus*

Makassar   [118 A5]
★ Mediterranean food in the Glockenbach district. The head chef was ship's cook to marine explorer Jacques Cousteau. He's got a knack for hot, spicy Creole cooking, too. *Daily 6 pm–1 am; Dreimühlenstrasse 25; Tel. 77 69 59; U-Bahn: 3/6, Sendlinger Tor; bus: 31, Ehrengutstrasse*

Punto Trentino   [110 C5]
Italian cooking, also from the Friaul region. Try the *strangolapreti* (priest stranglers) and think of Don Giovanni over a glass of Marzemino. *Mon–Fri 11.30 am–10 pm, Sat 11.30 am–3 pm; Sendlinger Strasse 62; Tel. 26 02 31 01; U-Bahn: 1/2/3/6, Sendlinger Tor*

Reitschule   [114 C5]
🏃 Haunt of pin-striped students of economics and the like. A little on the pretentious side. Best visited after a weekday afternoon stroll through the English Garden. *Daily 9 am–1 am; Königinstrasse 34; Tel. 388 87 60; U-Bahn: 3/6, Giselastrasse; bus: 54*

Rincón   [111 E5]
This former printing works is now the lovingly decorated setting for the chef's occasional, extravagant culinary fantasies. 'Rincón' means 'corner' in Spanish, a fitting name for this cornerstone in Munich's bistro landscape.. *Mon–Fri 9 am–1 am, Sat&Sun 10 am–1 am; Rumfordstrasse 34; Tel. 21 93 93 40; S-Bahn: Isartor*

Roma   [111 F3]
One of Munich's oldest star haunts. Decor and food take some getting used to, but the atmosphere is quite

unique. *Daily 8 am–3 am; Maximilianstrasse 31; Tel. 22 74 35; S-Bahn: Isartor*

Romagna Antica [114 A4]

Italian cuisine of very noble origin. *Mon–Thurs noon–2.30 pm, 7 pm to 11.30 pm, Fri&Sat 7 pm–11.30 pm; Elisabethstrasse 52; Tel. 271 63 55; U-Bahn: 2, Hohenzollernplatz; bus: 33*

Ruffini [113 D3]

🏃 Good, value-for-money restaurant, where the established artist breakfasts alongside the radio DJ. And in summer, they all enjoy the roof terrace. *Tues–Sun 10 am–midnight: Orffstrasse 22; Tel. 16 11 60; U-Bahn: 1, Rotkreuzplatz*

Rusticana [119 E3]

Munich's best spareribs compensate for the excessively rustic setting. Amusing mixture of American cooking and Haidhausen charm. *Tues–Thurs 6 pm–1 am, Fri&Sat 6 pm–3 am; Grillparzerstrasse 7; Tel. 470 38 87; U-Bahn: 4, Prinzregentenplatz*

Shoya [114 A6]

Friends of the land of the rising sun are in good hands here. Not particularly cheap, but the menu boasts pleasantly exotic dishes – and not just sushi. *Mon–Sat 11.30 am–2.30 pm, 6.30 pm–11.30 pm; Gabelsbergerstrasse 85; Tel. 523 62 49; U-Bahn: 2, Königsplatz*

Spices [119 D4]

Hotel bistros are not to everyone's taste. This one in the new Forum Hotel (formerly the Penta) is a mecca for fans of light cuisine, ranging from Asia to Italy – sounds daring, tastes terrific. *Daily noon–midnight; Hochstrasse 3; Tel. 48 03-0; S-Bahn: Rosenheimerstrasse*

Augustiner Grossgaststätten: sworn to uphold Bavarian tradition

Insider Tip Sum [111 D4]

The resourceful PR people from the department store Beck am Rathauseck have turned their attention to their customers' stomachs! Fine, Asian cuisine. The prices are on store level. *Mon–Fri 10 am–8 pm, Sat 10 am–4 pm; Marienplatz 2; Tel. 23 69 14 47; S- and U-Bahn: Marienplatz*

Werneckhof [115 D4]

Unusual, but good: French food in a Bavarian setting. *Daily 6 pm–midnight; Werneckstrasse 11; Tel. 39 99 36; U-Bahn: 3/6, Münchner Freiheit*

RESTAURANTS €

American Fried Chicken [116 B6]

In the fast-food battle between McDonald's and Burger King, they come off best. Fantastic chicken wings! Shame it's not more central. *Daily 11 am–11 pm; Ehrwalder Strasse 8; Tel. 71 14 24; U-Bahn: 6, Westpark; bus: 33, Garmischer Strasse*

Augustiner Grossgaststätten [110 C3]

Despite its position slap bang on the tourist trail, it remains an authentic, old-style beer hall serving good-quality food. The beer from Munich's oldest brewery is the proud symbol of a pub tradition reaching back to 1328. *Mon–Fri 9 am–midnight, Sat&Sun 10 am–midnight; Neuhauser Strasse 25–27; Tel. 23 18 32 57; S- and U-Bahn: Marienplatz or Stachus*

★ Blaues Haus [111 F4]

Dine just a stone's throw from the Kammerspiele and rub shoulders with the stars. The food is posh Bavarian and the atmosphere such that you'll gladly stay all evening. *Daily 11 am–1 am; Hildegardstrasse 1; Tel. 23 33 69 77; S- and U-Bahn: Marienplatz*

Braunauer Hof [111 E5]

Good, solid home cooking, in the best sense of the word, though for some, the decor is a little too rustic. *Mon–Sat 9 am–midnight; Frauenstrasse 42; Tel. 22 36 13; S-Bahn: Isartor*

1. Münchner Kartoffelhaus [111 E4]

If you want to know what you can do with a potato, besides fry it or boil it, then this is the place for you. Just work your way down the menu – and don't forget the sweet potatoes either! *Mon–Thurs noon to 11 pm, Fri&Sat noon–1 am, Sun 5.30 pm–11 pm; Hochbrückenstrasse 3; Tel. 29 63 31; U-Bahn: 3/6, Marienplatz*

Franziskaner Fuchsenstubn [111 E3]

★ In this time-honoured establishment, where the customer is king and hospitality is a byword, they say you'll find the best *Weisswurst* in town. Highly recommended: roast sucking pig in malt beer. *Daily 8 am–midnight; Perusastrasse 5; Tel. 231 81 20; S- and U-Bahn: Marienplatz*

Fraunhofer [110 C6]

★ 🏃 Munich's best-known student pub, drenched in '68 generation philosophy and beery nostalgia. *Daily 4 pm–1 am, Sept–Apr: Sun from 11 am; Fraunhoferstrasse 9; Tel. 26 64 60; U-Bahn: 1/2, Fraunhoferstrasse*

The one and only Hofbräuhaus

Garibaldi [114 B6]

Gourmet legend in Schwabing. Superb *hors d'oeuvres*, top-quality cheeses and Italian wines. *Mon–Fri 11 am–8 pm, Sat 10 am–4 pm; Schellingstrasse 60; Tel. 272 09 06; U-Bahn: 2, Theresienstrasse*

Hofbräuhaus [111 E4]

'In München steht ein …' Birthplace of the legendary drinking song. Home-made sweet mustard to go with the *Weisswurst*, gallons of beer, packed to the gills with tourists and locals. Live music provides genuine Bavarian cheer. *Daily 9 am–midnight; Am Platzl 9; Tel. 22 16 76; S- and U-Bahn: Marienplatz*

Isarbräu [120 B6]

Neo-traditional inn located in former Isartal station. Main attraction is the brewery next door. The beer is distinctive, the food is better-than-average Bavarian. *Daily 11 am to 1 am; Kreuzeckstrasse 23/Grosshesselohe; Tel. 79 89 61; S-Bahn: 7, Grosshesselohe*

Café Schmock [116 F1]

'Schmock' roughly means 'idiot' in Yiddish, but this certainly doesn't apply to the proprietors. They have discovered a real gap in the market: in this splendid old building they offer not only classic cocktails, but also have a fine selection of cigars, plus Israeli-Arabic-international cuisine. Not everything here is genuinely kosher, but the meat is from ritually slaughtered animals. *Daily 9 am–1 am; Augustenstrasse 52; Tel. 52 35 05 35; U-Bahn: 2, Josephsplatz*

Il Soprano [117 E6]

★ Undoubtedly Munich's best Italian restaurant for pasta and fish, right next to the wholesale market. Small, cramped, loud, *fantastico!* Try it – now! *Mon–Sat 10 am–1 am; Kochelseestrasse 8; Tel. 725 52 88; U-Bahn: 3/6, Implerstrasse*

Weinbauer [115 D4]
Insider Tip

Despite neo-Bavarian re-vamp, a pleasant restaurant, with good beer at reasonable prices. Lots of students. *Daily 11 am–1 am; Fendstrasse 5; Tel. 39 81 55; U-Bahn: 3/6, Münchner Freiheit*

Weisses Bräuhaus [111 E4]

★ Even after its complete overhaul, this is still a most convincing Bavarian pub, with grumpy but efficient waitresses and the most heavenly bread dumplings on earth. One classic Bavarian dish after another. *Daily 7 am–midnight; Tal 7; Tel. 29 98 75; S- and U-Bahn: Marienplatz*

Wirtshaus
Zum Straubinger [110 C6]

Formerly Straubinger Hof and best Bavarian restaurant in town. Under new management, turned country-style *Lederhosen* zone. The small, pretty beer garden compensates somewhat. *Daily 9 am–1 am; Blumenstrasse 5; Tel. 232 38 30; S- and U-Bahn: Marienplatz or Sendlinger Tor*

WINE BARS

Gandl [118 C2]

Once a grocery store, then a delicatessen. Now, you can buy and eat fantastic food here; in the daytime, light pasta dishes, in the evenings, more lavish items, with a hint of Paris. Prices on the high side, but realistic. There's even a 'three-minute dish' for people in a hurry!

Mon–Sat 9 am–12.30 am; Tel. 29 16 25 25; St-Anna-Platz 1; U-Bahn: 4/5, Lehel

Gourmets Garden [114 B5]
Insider Tip

Paradise for those who can do without meat, but not other epicurean delights. Meeting place of up-market vegetarians and vegans. *Mon–Fri 8.30 am–8 pm; Belgradstrasse 9; tram: 27, Kurfürstenplatz*

Walter & Benjamin [111 D5]

Fine wines from the most famous vineyards in Europe, plus a small selection of excellent dishes – here, specialists cook for specialists. *Tues–Fri 11 am–11 pm, Sat 10 am–11 pm; Rumfordstrasse 1; Tel. 26 02 41 74; S-Bahn: Isartor*

At the wine bars: a bite to eat and a gem from the wine cellar

Do it in style!

Fashion city Munich invites you on a shopping spree. There are plenty of beautiful and unusual items to be discovered

The busiest shopping streets in Munich's pedestrianised zone are *Neuhauser Strasse* and *Kaufingerstrasse* between Marienplatz and Stachus with the new Hypovereinsbank Passage and the 'Arcade'. A string of department stores, boutiques, jewellers and record shops unfolds. Pavement artists and musicians manage, if only for a moment, to distract their fellow creatures on their spending spree.

Catering to the highest of tastes

The second main pedestrianised shopping axis runs from Marienplatz to Odeonsplatz, and comes under the heading 'fat wallet'. In ★ *Theatinerstrasse,* the almost-complete *Fünf Höfen* (Five Courtyards) and the other pretty shopping arcades which branch off left and right, you'll find exquisite fashion boutiques, gentlemen's outfitters, milliners, Italian shoe shops, jewellers and art galleries. This exclusive patch extends from Perusastrasse and Residenzstrasse, right up to Briennerstrasse and Salvatorplatz. The Gärtnerplatzviertel has progressed from gay quarter to shopper's paradise for fans of exotic fashions, such as hemp clothing or

Fashion and more besides – every quarter has its own special style

daringly innovative tailored items. Not-so-enthusiastic co-shoppers can be parked in one of the countless cafés or sent to the hairdressers: the district boasts probably the world's highest proportion of *figaros*. Without a doubt *Maximilianstrasse* is Munich's No. 1 luxury shopping mile. Here, between the National Theatre and the old town ring road, you'll find only the heftiest price tags, whether it be for hunting gear, jewellery or art.

In recent years, ★ *Sendlinger Strasse* from Marienplatz up to Sendlinger Tor has developed into a pleasant shopping street, with many small shops selling goods at reasonable prices. It is also an alternative for those who find the pedestrianised zones too crowded and claustrophobic. Just before the Asamkirche, a shopping arcade links Sendlinger Strasse with

Kreuzstrasse: the *Asampassage,* an oasis in the city with cafés, pubs and shops. *Tal* is the name of the street between Marienplatz and Isartor, and offers tourists an interesting blend of shops selling anything from Bavarian-kitsch souvenirs to computers.

To track down *Zeitgeist* trends and way-out gear, you have to head out to Schwabing. Not Altschwabing, though, where you're more likely to get ripped off, but to the student area between *Leopoldstrasse,* ★ *Hohenzollernstrasse, Amalienstrasse,* ★ *Schellingstrasse* and *Türkenstrasse.* Fashions and fashion outlets change so quickly here, that it's best just to stroll around, look, enjoy and be inspired. The *Amalienpassage,* tucked away between the old, venerable houses behind the university, links Türkenstrasse and Amalienstrasse: small, idyllic cafés, chic boutiques, Asian and South American shops. Those on the lookout for cheap goods from the world of computers, should make for *Landwehrstrasse* close to Stachus.

Shops and department stores in the city centre are open as follows: Mon to Fri 9 am to 8 pm, on Saturdays until 4 pm only (outside the centre, generally only until 2 pm). The markets are open for business from 7.30 am or 8 am.

ANTIQUES & ANTIQUARIAN BOOKS

Antique shops are centred in Schwabing's Türkenstrasse, Barerstrasse and Briennerstrasse, around Promenadeplatz and in the side streets between the Viktualienmarkt and Isartor.

Antikpalast   [119 E5] Inside Tip

★ Whether Art Nouveau or Biedermeier, vase or bed, for 10 or for 1000 Euro, antiques freaks are sure to find something they don't necessarily need, but desperately want. Around 5000 sq m of showroom and over 100 dealers mean there's many a bargain to be had. *Thurs 2 pm–7 pm, Fri 10 am–7 pm, Sat 10 am–6 pm; Rosenheimer Strasse 143; S- and U-Bahn: Ostbahnhof*

Antiquariat Maxvorstadt I   [114 B6]

Worth highlighting among a multitude of similar dealers in the district. Specialist for books on Bavarian history. *Mon, Wed, Thurs, Fri 11.30 am–6 pm, Tues 1 pm–4 pm, Sat 11 am–1 pm; Schellingstrasse 32; U-Bahn: 3/6, Universität*

Gabriele Ruef   [110 C2]

First stop for South German folk art. Country antiques from the period before 1830. Delft tiles. *Ottostrasse 13 (Neuer Kunstblock); S- and U-Bahn: Stachus; tram: 18*

Ketterer   [119 E2]

Auctioneers for modern classics, Munich School and contemporary art. *Prinzregentenstrasse 61; U-Bahn: 4, Prinzregentenplatz*

Kunstauktionshaus Neumeister   [114 B6]

One of the most prestigious houses in the business. High-quality, fine antiques, sculptures, carpets, furniture, paintings and prints are put up for auction here, with the emphasis on old masters, works from the Munich School and 19th- and 20th-century pictures. *Barerstrasse 37; bus: 33; tram: 18*

MARCO POLO Highlights »Shopping«

★ **Viktualienmarkt**
Fresh wares to snack or to cook (page 68)

★ **Beck am Rathauseck**
Bags of original ideas in store (page 66)

★ **Hertie-Markthallen**
Insider Tip Shopping in the lap of luxury, and a lot cheaper than at the big-name delicatessens (page 67)

★ **Radspieler**
Fine arts and crafts as a design philosophy (page 67)

★ **Schellingstrasse**
Schwabing's shopping mecca, and no rubbish on sale either (page 64)

★ **Hohenzollernstrasse**
Same again, only more up-market (page 64)

★ **Theatinerstrasse**
Refined, but realistic (page 63)

★ **Dallmayr**
Temple of good taste, from Amaretto to Zabaione, plus fine coffees and tobacco. Luxury snack bar (page 65)

★ **Antikpalast**
Insider Tip Uninspiring hall, but a paradise for antiques freaks (page 64)

★ **Sendlinger Strasse**
Fashion for all budgets (page 63)

DELICATESSEN

Dallmayr [111 E3]
★ Munich's traditional, stylish delicatessen. On these historic premises, with their mighty marble columns, the gourmet will discover a veritable paradise full of delights: fresh salads, paté, lobster and salmon, a selection of 120 sausages and cooked meats, 250 varieties of cheese, plus game, poultry and meat. Not to mention fine teas and coffees, wines, exclusive tobacco, a marvellous confectionery department and many other exotic specialities. On the first floor is a gourmet restaurant. *Dienerstrasse 14–15; S- and U-Bahn: Marienplatz*

Garibaldi [114 B6]
Small delicatessen with original Italian specialities and highly personal atmosphere. Well-known for its excellent wines. Small stand-up snack bar. Several branches, the original is in *Schellingstrasse 60; U-Bahn: 3/6, Universität; bus: 53; tram: 18*

Käfer [119 E2]
Less prestigious, but in. And not just to shop at. Anyone who's anyone has Käfer deliver. Strong points are the broad selection of fish, wine and cheese (240 varieties from France, 150 from Italy). Käfer also puts on regular Italian and French 'weeks' and is famous for its tent on the Wies'n during the Oktoberfest.

Prinzregentenstrasse 73; U-Bahn: 4, Prinzregentenplatz; bus: 53; tram: 18

Anglia English Bookshop [114 C6]

This has to be the most chaotic book shop in the world. The staff still manage to locate whatever you ask for, or can at least get hold of it from somewhere in the English-speaking world. A real experience for bookworms! *Schellingstrasse 3; U-Bahn: 3/6, Universität*

Basic [111 E5]

Munich's first eco-store is a real winner. Top location, top-quality, certified goods, not overly 'green' atmosphere and a fine snack bar mean that Basic has thrown down the gauntlet to the 'Voll-Korner' chain of eco shops (for example at the corner of Volkartstrasse and Frunsbergstrasse). *Westenrieder-strasse 35; S- and U-Bahn: Marien-platz; Schleissheimer Strasse 156 to 162; U-Bahn: 2, Hohenzollernplatz*

Beck am Rathauseck [111 D4]

★ The store with a difference, established in 1861: Marienplatz wouldn't be the same without it. Original, witty, charming. Textile palace over six floors, on the corner with Dienerstrasse

At Beck's you'll find popular, good quality collections alongside a really large sock and button department, plus items by young fashion designers, exquisite hand-made chocolates, coffee bar and restaurant (Sum). The selection in the CD department in terms of classical, jazz and ethnic music is quite unique. The knowledgeable sales staff are without equal, nation-wide. *Marienplatz 11; S- and U-Bahn: Marienplatz*

Inside Tip

From Antiques to Junk

Outside the pedestrianised zones lurks the odd bargain

For example in Hohenzollernstrasse (Schwabing) between Leopoldstrasse and Elisabethplatz: from Boss to Benetton, the designer gear here is much cheaper than elsewhere. Alternatively, the area around Gärtnerplatz offers clothes made of hemp, acrylic paints for artists, extravagant Italian shoes and, of course, no end of sexy underwear – especially for him. Finding high-class junk in Fraunhoferstrasse is child's play. The latest shopping attraction are the Fünf Höfe (Five Courtyards), due to be completed at the end of 2003, but already a huge crowd-puller after the opening of the first construction phase. Alongside the new Hypo-Kunsthalle, more than 30 top-notch shops and eateries have opened up, for example *manufactum*, which sells high-quality everyday utensils, or *Charles Schumann's Tagesbar*.

Hertie am Bahnhof [110 A3]
This department store has been in Munich since 1905, and today is one of the biggest names in Germany. Apart from the usual range of goods, it also offers its own special ★ Hertie Market Hall for lovers of fine food, with a broad selection of wholefood items. *Bahnhofsplatz 7; S- and U-Bahn: Hauptbahnhof*

Manufactum [111 D2–3]
Since 2001 the Five Courtyards have been offering top-quality products of all kinds, including the goods at Peter Seewald's former monastery shop: everything which is manufactured in Bavarian monasteries. *Kardinal-Faulhaber-Strasse 11; U-Bahn: 3–6, Marienplatz or Odeonsplatz*

Radspieler [110 C4]
★ Up-market store in Hackenstrasse in the house of the same name. From designer potato peeler to Rolls Royce suitcase – only to be carried by liveried chauffeurs, of course. Radspieler F. & Co. has everything for the home – of the finest quality. The building on the opposite corner has folk art, textiles, ceramics, tableware and furniture. *Hackenstrasse 4 and 7; S- and U-Bahn: Marienplatz*

ART GALLERIES

Although the conservative metropolis on the Isar is no picnic for young, experimental artists, the city offers some 100 galleries selling an astonishingly broad palette of works. In typical Munich style, most of the big-name galleries have settled in and around Maximilianstrasse. (Every first Thursday in the month is late-night opening.) Schwabing's heyday as an artist's quarter is past. The most important galleries and exhibition rooms publish their own monthly brochure, available in each gallery. Check the listings magazines, such as *Munich Found* or *München im ...* for details of current exhibitions. The website *www.munich-online.de* gives a good overview under '*Musik + Kultur*': '*Galerien*'.

ARTS & CRAFTS

Antiquitäten Muggenthaler [110 C6]
Margit Muggenthaler is most certainly Munich's nicest professional junk dealer. Her speciality: Art-Nouveau clothing and chairs. *Generally 2 pm–6 pm only; Fraunhoferstrasse 1; U-Bahn: 1/2, Fraunhoferstrasse*

Bayerischer Kunstgewerbe-Verein [110 C3]
Three hundred art and craft workshops display and sell their wares here. Everything from mundane to avant-garde. *Pacellistrasse 6–8; S- and U-Bahn: Stachus; tram: 19*

Galerie Ruf [110 C5]
Alongside the usual Picasso prints and Christo pieces, you could turn up a real gem in the field of new art. *Tues–Fri 10.30 am–12.30 pm, 2 pm–6.30 pm, Sat 10.30 am–3 pm; Oberanger 35; U-Bahn: 1/2/3/6, Sendlinger Tor*

Künstlerwerkstatt Lothringer Strasse [119 D4]
Well-established avant-garde, exhibitions change every six weeks. On the first floor, media lab for computer art. Tip: next door sells works

Insider Tip

by young graduates of the Academy of Art. *Lothringer Strasse 13; S-Bahn: Rosenheimer Platz*

Das Landhauseck [111 D5]

One of the best sources of Bavarian wood and ceramic products. Even here, though, not everything is as old as it looks. The staff are knowledgeable, however, and you can be sure that the imitation decorative shelves and farmhouse cupboards are of a high standard. *At the corner of Corneliusstrasse and Prälat-Zistl-Strasse; S- and U-Bahn: Marienplatz*

Papyros [110 C4]

A huge selection of exquisite paper, ornate paperweights and hand-bound calendars. *Eisenmannstrasse 4; S- and U-Bahn: Marienplatz*

Wachszieher am Dom [111 D4]

Specialist candle shop, also selling waxen images. One of the last non-industrial candle manufacturers. *Sporerstrasse 2; S- and U-Bahn: Marienplatz*

MARKETS & FLEA MARKETS

Munich has little left to offer flea market fans. The days of the huge flea markets are officially over, especially since the Dachauer-Hallen – formerly a junk-lover's paradise at the weekends – were torn down in 1989. You can still get hold of a few knick-knacks at lunchtimes around the large *Unimensa* (university cafeteria) in *Giselastrasse* [114 C5], and the market on Fridays and Saturdays from 7 am to 6 pm at the *Kunstpark Ost* [119 E5] in *Grafinger Strasse 6 (S- and U-Bahn: Ostbahnhof)* is also popular.

Elisabethmarkt [114 B4] *Inside Tip*

Small-scale, but with a cosy atmosphere. Few tourists make it to this corner of Schwabing. The market on Elisabethplatz is a treasured remnant of traditional Schwabing family life. On sale are fruit and vegetables, cheese, fish and poultry, plus flowers. *Daily, except Sun; Elisabethplatz; U-Bahn: 2, Hohenzollernplatz; tram: 18*

Markt am Wiener Platz [119 D3]

Small, down-to-earth market in Haidhausen with a handful of stands, which have been run by the same families for decades. Close to the Hofbräukeller (fine beer garden) and only 100 m away from the State Parliament, both market and surrounding area are worth a visit. The Wiener Platz café on the corner of Steinstrasse is the place to be. Highly recommended is also a stroll along Steinstrasse to Rosenheimer Platz: a few off-beat shops (second-hand, 1950s 'antiques', etc.). *Daily, except Sun; U-Bahn: 4/5, Max-Weber-Platz*

Viktualienmarkt [111 D5]

★ The largest and oldest food market in Munich, established in 1807, and just a stone's throw from Marienplatz. Up for grabs are fruit, vegetables, herbs, flowers, dairy products, eggs, poultry, wine, bread and honey. Indoors there's fish, meat and game. The market still radiates that typical Munich informality and charm, and you might come across a real character among the stallholders. The butchers have their own row of stands in the arcade below the Petersberg. The Viktualienmarkt is synonymous with high quality and high prices.

Watch out for the Munich Brewer's Association maypole, the small beer garden, six memorial fountains with statues of Bavarian folk singers, comedians and humorists. Almost every day sees Karl Valentin and co. with a fresh bunch of flowers in their arms. *Daily, except Sun 7.30 am–6 pm; S- and U-Bahn: Marienplatz*

FASHION

The fashion business looked to Munich for many years, and not just with regard to traditional costume, the *Tracht*. However, since the fashion weeks in spring and autumn no longer take place, there are only a few specialist shows focusing on country wear and sportswear. As home to the much sought-after school of fashion design on the Rossmarkt and a huge pool of young, keen shoppers with money to spare, it's not surprising that you will find just about anything money can buy in Munich's boutiques.

All About Eve [111 D6]

Tailor-made dreams on sale here! When the Oscar ceremony looms, the shop does a particularly brisk trade. Designer Adrian Runhof is well known for his reproductions of the evening gowns of such stars as Julia Roberts – at affordable prices, to boot. A truly sensational shop with its own couture collection, individually altered on request. *Klenzestrasse 41; U-Bahn: 1/2, Fraunhoferstrasse*

Jeans-Kaltenbach [110 C4]

Its most powerful sales argument to this day is its claim to be the largest

Probably Germany's most famous market: the Viktualienmarkt

jeans shop in the world. Several floors of brand-name jeans, shirts and jackets in all sizes, colours and price classes. Plus anything which remotely goes with jeans, such as belts, boots, etc. *Herzogspitalstrasse 4, close to Altheimer Eck; S- and U-Bahn: Marienplatz*

Karl Wagner [111 E4]

The specialist dealers in *Lederhosen*. Whether short or long, of cowhide, elk or deerskin, plain or colourfully embroidered – they're all here. Made-to-measure, they'll set you back between 250 and 750 Euro. *Tal 7; S- and U-Bahn: Marienplatz*

Loden-Frey [111 D3]

Munich's biggest specialist outlet for *Loden* and other traditional costumes has long since made a name for itself outside its Bavarian homeland. They stock just about everything you can think of: from the corresponding shoes down to the good old *Lodenjanker* (traditional Tyrolean jacket – right back in fashion, albeit pepped up a little) and the *Gamsbarthut* (felt hat with tuft of chamois hair).

In addition, you'll also find English, French and Italian model designs and lots of accessories. *Maffeistrasse 7–9 (directly behind the Frauenkirche); S- and U-Bahn: Marienplatz*

Lust auf Mode [113 D3]

A small shop for young people with plenty of pocket money on hand. Almost all the big names in the fashion industry are to be had here, often at drastically reduced prices. *Leonrodstrasse 6; U-Bahn: 1, Rotkreuzplatz*

Nicowa [110 C5] Inside Tip

Small but very impressive boutique in Sendlinger Strasse, offering for the most part elegant, young fashions from its own designer team. Their slogan 'We'll show you the future' is possibly a little optimistic, but they've certainly got enough to see you through the next cocktail party! *Sendlinger Strasse 46; S- and U-Bahn: Sendlinger Tor*

Toccata [111 D6]

No, it has nothing to do with music, but is rather a little treasure trove of up-to-date women's wear in linen, silk and, especially in summer, hemp. Perfect service, and a shining example of what makes this district so attractive to shoppers. Surprise package for men on the lookout for a present, who also know the size of the lady in question. *Klenzestrasse 38; U-Bahn: 1/2, Fraunhoferstrasse*

Tracht und Heimat [110 C5]

The name says it all: the true-blue Bavarian comes here to order his made-to-measure *Tracht* – not exactly cheap, but original. *Oberanger 9; S- and U-Bahn: Sendlinger Tor*

SHOES

Eduard Meier [111 E3]

Germany's oldest shoe shop, purveyor to the court since 1596. His visiting card reads 'Fine Shoes, Hunting Suits, Flyfishing'. *Residenzstrasse 22; S- and U-Bahn: Marienplatz or U-Bahn: 3/4/5/6, Odeonsplatz*

Face [110 C4]

Don't be misled by the name; they only sell shoes. Not just any old shoes, but Doc Martens and other clumpy footwear. Huge selection and pretty freaky. *Altheimer Eck 3; S- and U-Bahn: Marienplatz*

Outdoor Schuhe [117 F4]

Those who decide on a spontaneous trip into the mountains, will find the appropriate footwear here. Excellent service and reasonable prices, plus a few tips for the planned hike thrown in. *Kapuzinerplatz: U-Bahn: 3/6, Goetheplatz*

Stilettos or Doc Martens: Munich's got them all

MISCELLANEOUS

Bears & Friends [114 B5]

Heaven on earth for the sweet-toothed who are crazy about those colourful little jelly bears. A mouth-watering selection of around 100 different shapes, colours and flavours! *Schellingstrasse 42; U-Bahn: 3/6, Universität*

British Shop [114 A5]

For Anglophiles, those who get homesick on holiday and people in need of a Munich's largest stockist of British groceries and other odds and ends. *Schellingstrasse 100; U-Bahn: Theresienstrasse*

Et cetera [111 F3]

Karl Valentin could have been the inspiration behind this shop: a collection of original Bavarian curios and charming, but crazy odds and ends. There's a Bavarian globe, for example, and a clock which runs backwards. *Wurzerstrasse 12 (exactly 111 paces from the Vier Jahreszeiten Hotel); S- and U-Bahn: Marienplatz*

Film Oldies [110 C6]

Treasure trove for cineastes and nostalgic film freaks. You can buy, sell or borrow film posters. They have books about films, cinema programmes, autographs and still photos from over 50 years of cinema history. *Mon–Fri 1.30 pm–6.30 pm, Sat 11 am–3 pm; Müllerstrasse 46; U-Bahn: Sendlinger Tor*

Nymphenburger Porzellan [111 E2]

It may seem a little strange to find Bavaria's most prestigious porcelain listed in the 'Miscellaneous' section, but quality and price are proof that we are dealing with something rather unique in this case. The showroom exudes an air of luxury and long tradition (production goes back as far as 1747). It doesn't have to be a complete dinner service, a tiny, exquisite cup would probably suffice. *Odeonsplatz 1; U-Bahn: 3/6, Odeonsplatz*

The Tiger Store [118 C4]

Furnishings, clothing – you name it, if you can fit a few tiger stripes on it, you'll find it here. Don't worry, either; everything is strictly imitation. And what's more, part of the profits go to the World Wildlife Fund. *Lilienstrasse 7, S-Bahn: Rosenheimer Platz*

Sleep well!

**From luxury hotels to cosy, affordable guest houses –
Munich has all you need for that good night's sleep**

Like any self-respecting metropolis, Munich is not short of outrageously luxurious accommodation. Lesser mortals should also be warned: Munich is by no means cheap, especially in periods of high demand, such as during the Oktoberfest or the major trade fairs. Do not despair, though. In addition to the famous palatial hotels, Munich also has plenty of medium-sized and small hotels and guest houses, offering ample capacity.

Choose a hotel with good links to the public transport network. Driving and parking in the city centre only mean unnecessary stress. Information on hotels and booking rooms is available from the accommodation service of the tourist information offices, or you can book yourself by phone or via the internet. In the case of larger hotels, have your credit card number ready. Hotels often have special offers, but only if you ask specifically!

Many hotels are listed under the following internet addresses: *www. deutschland-hotel.de/muc/muenchen.htm, www.muenchen-tourist. de or www.nethotels.com*. There is a string of cheap hotels in Schillerstrasse, south of the main railway station.

*One of the top addresses:
the Vier Jahreszeiten Hotel*

HOTELS €€€

Ambassador Park Hotel [117 D5]
Apartment-style accommodation, convenient for the zoo. 80 beds. *Plinganserstrasse 102; Tel. 72 48 90; Fax 72 48 91 00; S-Bahn: 7/27; U-Bahn: 6, Harras*

Holiday Inn [114 C3]
First-class international hotel offering comprehensive service in northern Schwabing. Two restaurants, two bars, swimming pool in Roman ambience. 653 beds. *Leopoldstrasse 194; Tel. 38 17 90; Fax 38 17 98 88; U-Bahn: 3/6, Münchner Freiheit; bus: 43, 85*

Insel-Mühle [0]
★ Hotel in Untermenzing, west of the city centre. A beautifully restored old building with an ultra-modern marketing concept. Many seasonal special offers, with an overnight stay plus ticket (e. g. for a musical) from 120 Euro. 76 beds. *Von-Kahr-Strasse 87; Tel. 810 10; Fax 812 05 71; S-Bahn: 2, Allach*

König Ludwig [114 C4]
★ Distinguished, small hotel in the heart of Schwabing. Very personal atmosphere, extremely quiet, although only a three-minute walk from Münchner Freiheit. Hopeless romantics should book room 62: a

maisonette suite with roof terrace and open fireplace. 80 beds. *Hohenzollernstrasse 3; Tel. 33 59 95; Fax 39 46 58; U-Bahn: 3/6, Münchner Freiheit*

Opéra [118 C2]

★ Intimate and stylish hotel in Lehel, painstakingly renovated to perfection by the previous owner. Even under new ownership, a wonderful combination of elegance and privacy. Bavarian National Museum and English Garden within easy walking distance. 28 beds. *St-Anna-Strasse 10; Tel. 22 55 33; Fax 22 55 38; U-Bahn: 4/5, Lehel*

Das Palace München [119 E2]

★ Top address, lovingly designed interior – a tip for (well-to-do) individualists. 125 beds. *Trogerstrasse 21; Tel. 41 97 10; Fax 41 97 18 19; U-Bahn: 4, Prinzregentenplatz*

Park Hilton [115 D6]

Like all Hilton Hotels, this one offers all creature comforts: two restaurants, bar and Cigar Lounge, wellness area, boutiques and hairdresser. Situated close to the English Garden. The newer City Hilton in Haidhausen is every bit as luxurious. Both hotels have 479 beds. *Am Tucherpark 7; Tel. 384 50; Fax 38 45 25 88; U-Bahn: 4/5, Lehel*

Preysing [119 D3]

Elegant hotel close to the Gasteig Culture Centre. 95 beds. *Preysingstrasse 1; Tel. 45 84 50; Fax 45 84 54 44; S-Bahn: Rosenheimer Platz*

Torbräu [111 F5]

There's been a hotel here since 1490. Surprisingly modern interior. Refined, discreet. 156 beds. *Tal 41; Tel. 24 23 40; Fax 24 23 42 35; www.torbraeu.de; S-Bahn: Isartor*

Deutsches Theater [110 A4]

Informally run hotel with a pleasant, personal atmosphere in central city location. Part of the entertainment complex around the Deutsches Theater. Ideal for culture fans, sights within easy reach. All the rooms are furnished in Laura Ashley style. 56 beds. *Landwehrstrasse 18; Tel. 545 85 25; Fax 54 58 52 61; S- and U-Bahn: Stachus*

Leopold [114 C3]

★ Pleasant hotel. Tip: book a room overlooking the inner courtyard. 100 beds. *Leopoldstrasse 119; Tel. 36 70 61; Fax 36 04 31 50; U-Bahn: 3/6, Münchner Freiheit*

Hotel Luise [116 C6]

Somewhat outside the centre, but still well placed, in a pleasant residential area with U-Bahn connection. 18 beds. *Luise-Kiesselbach-Platz 32; Tel. 719 10 87; Fax 719 42 42; U-Bahn: 6, Westpark*

Hotel Maria [117 E3]

Its location makes this an ideal place for Oktoberfest visitors – early booking absolutely essential. 160 beds. *Schwanthalerstrasse 112 to 114; Tel. 51 08 26; Fax 50 55 20; www.hotelmaria.de; U-Bahn: 4/5, Theresienwiese*

Mercure München Königin Elisabeth [113 E5]

★ Large hotel, acceptable prices, located in pleasant Neuhausen. 110 beds. *Leonrodstrasse 79a; Tel.*

12 68 60; Fax 12 68 64 59; U-Bahn: 1, Rotkreuzplatz

Insider Tip **Olympic** [110 C6]

★ Charming hotel, recommended for those who wish to live in style in one of the most attractive districts in the city. The mixture of English colonial style and Glockenbachviertel is irresistible. 54 beds. *Hans-Sachs-Strasse 4; Tel. 23 18 90; Fax 23 18 91 99; U-Bahn: 2/4, Fraunhoferstrasse*

Queens Hotel [115 F5]

Well-known conference hotel in the northeast of the city. 301 beds. *Effnerstrasse 99; Tel. 92 79 80; Fax 98 38 13; U-Bahn: 4, Arabellapark*

Wallis [110 A4]

A family-run hotel with welcoming, Swiss atmosphere, between the main railway station and the Theresienwiese, featuring 22 rooms in sober, business style and 32 rooms with typical Alpine decor. 104 beds. *Schwanthalerstrasse 8; Tel. 549 02 90; Fax 54 90 29 28; S- and U-Bahn: Stachus*

Wetterstein [0]

On Wettersteinplatz in Obergiesing, a working-class district which is turning chic. Excellent transport links. There's also a sauna, mud and steam baths. 110 beds. *Grünwalderstrasse 16; Tel. 697 00 25; Fax 69 43 45; U-Bahn: 1, Wettersteinplatz*

HOTELS €

Blauer Bock [111 D5]

★ Right in the centre of town on the Viktualienmarkt. Recommended

MARCO POLO **Highlights** »Accommodation«

★ **Das Palace München**
For the moneyed individualist (page 74)

★ **Insel-Mühle**
Peripheral idyll for connoisseurs (page 73)

★ **Mercure München Königin Elisabeth**
In Neuhausen, noble (page 74)

★ **Königshof**
Central, yet distinguished (page 76)

★ **Leopold**
Ask for a room on the inner courtyard (page 74)

★ **Opéra**
Insider Tip Small, noble, central, quiet (page 74)

★ **Olympic**
Insider Tip Colonial style in Glockenbachviertel (page 75)

★ **DJH Burg Schwaneck**
One of the most attractive youth hostels (page 77)

★ **Blauer Bock**
Cheap, but cosy (page 75)

★ **König Ludwig**
Super suite with open fireplace (page 73)

Luxury Hotels in Munich

Bayerischer Hof [111 D3]
Beautiful Classicist building in the heart of the city, haunt of the rich and famous. Special offers nevertheless. 711 beds; from 271–399 Euro, most expensive suite: 1439 Euro; *Promenadeplatz 2; Tel. 212 00; Fax 212 09 06; S- and U-Bahn: Stachus*

City Hilton [119 D4]
Architecturally, no better than the Gasteig, but luxurious hotel for that business trip. Occasional discounts. 952 beds; from 160–395 Euro; *Rosenheimer Strasse 15; Tel. 480 40; Fax 48 04 48 04; S-Bahn: Rosenheimer Platz*

Kempinski Hotel Vier Jahreszeiten [111 F3]
Rated the best hotel in town. Director von Treskow is busy trying to maintain the hotel's reputation, after accusations of having rested on its laurels for too long. Bar pianist Simon Schott is still the best in the world, though. 572 beds; from 335–485 Euro, most expensive suite: 1200 Euro; *Maximilianstrasse 17; Tel. 212 50; Fax 21 25 20 00; S- and U-Bahn: Marienplatz*

★ Königshof [110 B3]
Privately owned luxury hotel with star-rated cuisine, marble bathrooms: the No. 1 for connoisseurs. The Geisel family also runs Geisel's Vinothek round the corner. 170 beds; from 260–350 Euro, suite: 650 Euro; *Karlsplatz 25; Tel. 55 13 60; Fax 55 13 61 13; S- and U-Bahn: Stachus*

Mandarin Oriental [111 F4]
New hotel within magnificent, old walls. The former Antikhaus was turned into luxury hotel. The expert's favourite. Chosen stop-over for those with no money worries or extremely large expense accounts. Fine food, plus a pool on the roof. 146 beds; from 330–420 Euro, suite: up to 1070 Euro; *Tel. 29 09 80; Fax 22 25 39; Neuturmstrasse 1; S- and U-Bahn: Marienplatz*

for those on a tight budget, or with a drop of Scottish blood in their veins. Here, you really do get what you pay for, which is not always true in Munich. 115 beds. *Sebastiansplatz 9; Tel. 23 17 80; Fax 23 17 82 00; S- and U-Bahn: Marienplatz*

Dachs [114 B6]
Family-run hotel in Schwabing. 90 beds. *Amalienstrasse 12; Tel. 28 20 86; Fax 28 08 29; U-Bahn: 3/4/5/6, Odeonsplatz*

Landsberger Hof [0]
In Pasing, handy for the 'Pasinger Fabrik' cultural centre. In summer, there's a pleasant beer garden, in winter, a cosy restaurant with open fireplace. 36 beds. *Bodenseestrasse 32; Tel. 88 18 05; Fax 834 04 26; S-Bahn: Pasing*

Monachia [117 F2]
Centrally located, bed and breakfast hotel. More comfortable than the surroundings would suggest. 70

beds. *Senefelderstrasse 3; Tel. 55 52 81; Fax 59 25 98; S- and U-Bahn: Hauptbahnhof*

Hotel Peter im Park [0]

Pasing is not that far out of town, and, what's more, this pretty suburb boasts the culture centre Pasinger Fabrik and an S-Bahn connection. 29 beds. *Neufeldstrasse 20; Tel. 88 13 56; Fax 83 08 41; S-Bahn: Pasing; bus: 43, Am Knie*

BED & BREAKFAST

Under *www.bed-and-breakfast.de*, you'll find cheap accommodation offers, even by Munich's standards, mostly in private houses. Up-to-date offers also via the agency of the same name. *Single room: 34–54 Euro, double room: 53–80 Euro; Tel. 76 99 69 00 (1 pm–5 pm); Fax 76 99 69 01*

FOR YOUNG PEOPLE

Accommodation offered in houses affiliated to the DJH (German Youth Hostels Association) is reserved for guests under 26 years of age.

Christlicher Verein Junger Menschen [118 A3]

🏃 The Young Men's Christian Association gives you a warm welcome. 85 beds. *Single: from 30 Euro, double: from 25 Euro per person; Landwehrstrasse 13; Tel. 552 14 10; info@cvjmmuenchen. org; S- and U-Bahn: Stachus*

DJH Burg Schwaneck [0]

★ 🏃 World-famous, in the south of Munich, with sauna. 130 beds in 4-, 6- and 8-bed dormitories. *Groups: full board from 22 Euro; Pul-lach, Burgweg 4–6; Tel. 793 06 43; S-Bahn: 7, Pullach*

DJH Jugendgästehaus [0]

🏃 Close to the zoo. Don't forget your YHA pass! 352 beds. *Per person: 19.20 Euro; Miesingstrasse 4; Tel. 723 65 60; jhmuenchen@djh-bayern.de; U-Bahn: 3, Thalkirchen*

DJH München [112 C5–6]

🏃 Close to the city centre. Don't forget your YHA pass! 385 beds. *Wendl-Dietrich-Strasse 20; B&B: 19.20 Euro; Tel. 13 11 56; jhmuen chen@dhj-bayern.de; U-Bahn: 1, Rotkreuzplatz*

4 you [117 F2]

To the north of the main railway station. Wholemeal food, quiet location. Open 24 hours a day. Child care in the house. 195 beds. *Dormitory bed per person: 16.50–35 Euro; Hirtenstrasse 18; Tel. 552 16 60; info @the4you.de; S- and U-Bahn: Hauptbahnhof*

Haus International [114 A4]

🏃 Rated the 'most popular youth meeting place in Germany', with swimming pool and disco. 550 beds. *Double: 26 Euro, 5-bed room: from 23 Euro, single: from 30 Euro; Elisabethstrasse 87; Tel. 12 00 60; info@haus-international.de; U-Bahn: 2, Hohenzollernplatz*

Kapuzinerhölzl [0] *Insider Tip*

Known the world over among young tourists simply as 'The Tent'. From 31 May to 31 August. Accommodation in large tents. Bring your own inflatable mattress. Typical price: in the main tent, 8.50 Euro including standard breakfast. *www.the-tent.de*

Munich shines – especially at night

Munich has a glittering cultural and nightlife programme for every taste

Village of a million inhabitants' or metropolis? A frequently asked question and not an easy one to answer. Munich does have a dizzyingly varied selection of bars, pubs, music venues, discos, cinemas and late-night cafés. The locals, however, still complain that the city basically shuts up shop at midnight. Don't worry, though, it's not quite as bad as all that. If you do a little research beforehand, have enough stamina (to deal with the bouncers), are adventurous enough (to discover what and why is currently *le dernier cri* and react accordingly), and have got cash to spare, we are convinced you won't find it too difficult to amuse yourself until the early hours. The most popular entertainment hot-spots: Schwabing (favourite with the over-25s), Haidhausen (risen from student quarter to yuppie zone), Neuhausen (intact world with little surprises), Schlachthofviertel (not yet renovated) and the Kunstpark Ost (target of the under-25s). Be warned: dead cert tips can be out again from one day to the next!

Not far from the Hofbräuhaus, but a world apart: the always full-to-bursting Bar Centrale

BARS

Bar Centrale [111 E4] *Insider Tip*

Not far from the Hofbräuhaus, and yet a world away. Typifies the best in Italian bars, with charming, slightly worn furniture, Campari and dreams of the sea. Snacks at lunchtime and in the evenings, and packed to the gills with eminently good-looking folk. *Mon–Sat 8 am to 1 am, Sun 10 am–1 am; Ledererstrasse 23; S- and U-Bahn: Marienplatz*

Bar Tabacco [110 C3] *Insider Tip*

When it comes to mixing cocktails, Edmond, Stefan and Yasar demonstrate what they learned as waiters under Charles Schumann – and it was worth the effort. No frills, elegant, tasteful bar atmosphere. *Mon to Thurs 5 pm–1 am, Fri&Sat 5 pm to 3 am; Hartmannstrasse 8; S- and U-Bahn: Stachus or Marienplatz*

Café Glockenspiel [111 D4]

Not just good for a coffee, but also a bar and restaurant with Vodka Sour and reasonable meals. The roof garden with the automatic folding roof is heaven! *Insider Tip Daily 10 am to 1 am; Marienplatz 28; U-Bahn: Marienplatz*

Hong Kong Bar [118 A5]

Relaxed atmosphere, wonderful Mai-Tais, remarkably attentive service and exquisite Far-Eastern cuisine. *Sun–Thurs 6 pm–1 am, Fri&Sat 6 pm–3 am; Kapuzinerstrasse 39; U-Bahn: 3/6, Goetheplatz; bus: 31, Kapuzinerstrasse*

Islay [118 C3]

No fancy cocktails here! A must for lovers of fine whisky. More than 150 types of this delicious refreshment, plus expert advice on choosing. We recommend trying two different 'wee drams', in preference to one double. *Daily 5 pm–1 am; Thierschstrasse 14; S-Bahn: Isartor*

Ksar [110 C6]

★ Lively and loud. Man seeks woman/man and vice-versa. The Whisky Sour is supposedly the best in town. The music is futuristic. *Daily 9 pm–3 am; Müllerstrasse 31; U-Bahn: 1/2/3/6, Sendlinger Tor*

'L-Bar' [111 F3]

Formerly top-notch restaurant Chesa, now dedicated to the fine art of cocktail mixing. The clientele matches the scene outside. Colonial flair, leather, the scent of fine cigar smoke and choice, small dishes. Ernst Lechthaler's Lechthaler AG is Germany's first gastronomic joint-stock company. *Mon–Sat 5 pm to 3 am; Wurzerstrasse 18; S- and U-Bahn: Marienplatz*

Lizard Lounge [111 E6]

Currently the only place to be. So packed, you can hardly take a breath, let alone a seat. Here, you find a mixture of creative people, both of the would-be variety and those content to watch. *Daily 7 pm to 1 am; Corneliusstrasse 34; U-Bahn: 1/2, Fraunhoferstrasse*

Nachtcafé [110 C2]

★ Unfortunately too many people have cottoned on to the fact that this is the best that Munich has to offer after 1 am. Night owl ambience with occasional legendary jazz sessions. *Daily 9 pm–6 am; Maximiliansplatz 5; S- and U-Bahn: Stachus*

Nage & Sauge [119 D3]

You've hardly room to gnaw ('Nagen') anything – but if you do, it's Italian. On the other hand, you can easily absorb ('Saugen') one of the young, light wines from the wood. In bar with the air of a crowded living room after 10 pm – take a slice of that atmosphere! *Daily 5.30 pm to 1 am; Mariannenstrasse 2; U-Bahn: 4/5, Lehel*

Padres Havanna Exit [111 D5]

Well-established on the ever-changing Munich bar scene, they probably serve the best Margaritas in town, accompanied by a groove somewhere between classic black and Salsa. *Sun–Thurs 7 pm–3 am, Fri&Sat 7 pm–4 am; Blumenstrasse 43; U-Bahn: 1/2/3/6, Sendlinger Tor*

Schumann's [111 F3]

★ Munich's No. 1 'American bar', where it is definitely not the done thing to wave if you spot the likes of Boris Becker or Klaus Maria Brandauer on the other side of the room. Serves the best Bloody Mary between Moscow and Paris. Many's the bar-propping society journalist who's said of Schumann's, 'I'd rather have a good Gimlet than a bad Hamlet.' *Mon–Fri 5 pm to*

3 am, Sun 6 pm–3 am; Maximilianstrasse 36; S-Bahn: Isartor

DISCOS

Insider Tip
Crash [114 B–C4]
Last bastion of heavy-metal and hard rockers, where the AC/DC and Led Zeppelin evergreens live on. Obligatory long manes, hard drinks, fair prices and a well-established suburban cattle market. *Thurs 8 pm–1 am, Fri&Sat 9 pm–4 am; Ainmillerstrasse 10; U-Bahn: 3/6, Giselastrasse*

Insider Tip
kafe KULT [0]
Founded ten years ago by young, hip people for young, hip people, and despite many bureaucratic hur-dles, still going strong. Munich's most extravagant dance venue, where the P1 and Pacha crowds are guaranteed to feel out of place. Generally weekends only. *Oberföhringer Strasse 156; www.kafekult.de; bus: 88, 90*

Nachtwerk [116 C2] **Insider Tip**
Popular dance club in a rather dreary area. Three in one: 'Normal folk' gather in the *Tanzlokal*, the *nachtwerkhalle* caters for the hip-hop, way-out crowd and the *Club* features After-work on Thursdays. *Fri&Sat 10.30 pm–4 am, in the summer holidays also Tues; Landsberger Strasse 185; www.nachtwerk.de; S-Bahn: Friedenheimer Brücke; tram: 19*

MARCO POLO **Highlights** »Entertainment«

★ **P1**
No. 1 disco – whoever's in here, is 'in' – or so they think (page 82)

★ **Pacha**
Tough competition for P1 from the Ibiza outpost (page 82)

★ **Muffathalle**
Insider Tip
Great cultural programme and a great place to get stranded (page 87)

★ **Café Zweistein**
Idyllic little café, inside and out (page 85)

★ **Nachtcafé**
Full to bursting with insiders, great music till 5 am (page 80)

★ **Kunstpark Ost**
Bars and clubs from cool to spaced-out (page 83)

★ **Wirtshaus im Schlachthof**
Rock music at its hottest (page 88)

★ **Lach- & Schiessgesellschaft**
Germany's oldest cabaret, presented by some new faces (page 82)

★ **Schumann's**
Fine for those who don't turn a hair at the sight of Boris (page 80)

★ **Ksar**
In terms of relationships, tolerance is the key (page 80)

P 1   [118 C1]

★ Munich's landmark noble disco, for people who are beautiful enough to convince the 'style police' on the door that they absolutely must get in! From around midnight, this is the ultimate 'see and be seen' stomping ground. *Sun–Fri 11 pm–4 am, Sat until 6 am; Prinzregentenstrasse 1; U-Bahn: 3/6, Odeonsplatz*

Pacha   [119 E5]

★ The market leadership of P1 is under threat. Competition comes in the shape of Pacha. The prototype is in Ibiza, the Munich-East branch is well on the way to becoming the top dog on the scene. Boris Becker might just pop in for a change; some New-Economy yuppie might rent the place and splash out 150,000 Euro for a party. Don't miss the famous After-Work Parties on Tuesdays and Wednesdays from 6 pm. Weekends are to be avoided. *Thurs 10 pm–4 am, Fri&Sat 10 pm to 5 am; Rosenheimer Strasse 145h; S- and U-Bahn: Ostbahnhof*

A touch of Ibiza in Munich: the Pacha

Parkcafé   [110 B2]

Famous for parties with names such as 'Hairdresser's Catapult' and 'Superhero's Tour', the Parkcafé is keen to hold its third-place ranking in the city charts. As you'd expect, the bouncers are unfriendly, to say the least. No trainers, no moustaches – unless your girlfriend flirts outrageously with the gorilla on the door! *Daily 11 pm–4 am; Sophienstrasse 7; S- and U-Bahn: Stachus*

CABARET

Drehleier   [119 D4] *Inside Tip*

Likeable cabaret bar with often hilarious programme. Amateurs still get a look in, too. Several times a year, the Drehleiter is the venue for the 'Varieté Spectaculum' – don't miss it. *Rosenheimer Strasse 123; Tel. 48 27 42; S-Bahn: Rosenheimer Strasse*

Hinterhoftheater   [O] *Inside Tip*

Situated in the working-class district of Hart, top-class repertoire of German-language artists. Drop in at the Wirtshaus am Hart for a beer after the show. *Sudetendeutsche Strasse 40; Tel. 311 60 39; tram: 12/13*

Jörg Maurers Unterton   [114 B5]

Cabaret artist Maurer is his own boss. Treasure trove of political cabaret gems. *Kurfürstenstrasse 8; Tel. 33 39 33; U-Bahn: 3/6, Universität; tram: 27*

Lach- & Schiessgesellschaft   [115 D4]

★ With a name like this (something like 'Laughing and Shooting Company'), they're onto a winner. A nation-wide household name when it comes to top-quality politi-

Kunstpark Ost

If it's not here,
it won't be anywhere

The site near the Ostbahnhof [119 E4–5], once occupied by a potato processing factory, has been home to ★ Europe's biggest disco and club complex since 1995. Big concert halls (Babylon, Colosseum), surrounded by hundreds of small bars and clubs featuring every possible music trend from hip-hop via ambient to retro and eso. Great during the week, to be avoided at weekends, when half of Munich seems to descend on the site. Among the newest clubs are *Raum 8* (fairly cool, female bouncer), *Stereo* with three bars on three levels (chart hits) and *the dome*, rather spaced-out, with coffins, funereal candles and crazy cocktails (free admission, drinks voucher). The future of the Kunstpark is uncertain. Probably safe until the end of 2003, it will then have to give way to redevelopment. *Grafinger Strasse 6; Tel. 49 00 29 28; www.kunstpark.de; all S-Bahn lines; U-Bahn: 5*

cal cabaret. Recently re-formed ensemble continues to pack in the crowds, sardine-style. *Haimhauser/Ursulastrasse; Tel. 39 19 97; U-Bahn: 3/6, Münchner Freiheit*

Theater im Fraunhofer [110 C6]
Backyard cabaret theatre with select programme. The cabaret elite premiere here; getting hold of tickets can be difficult. *Fraunhoferstrasse 9; Tel. 26 78 50; U-Bahn: 1/2, Fraunhoferstrasse*

CINEMAS

The following cinemas show Sunday matinées, mostly classical theatre and opera films. Phone for details. *Theatiner Film (Tel. 23 31 83), Tivoli (Tel. 26 43 26), Museumslichtspiele, Filmtheater Sendlinger Tor (Tel. 55 46 36), Film-Casino (Tel. 22 08 18) and Studio Isabella (Tel. 271 88 44).*

Cinema [113 F6]
Excellent art-house cinema with superb sound quality. Famous for its double features. Also English films daily. *Nymphenburger Strasse 31; Tel. 55 52 55; U-Bahn: 1, Stiglmaierplatz*

Filmmuseum [110 C5] Insider Tip
Film experts have put together a universally acclaimed film archive. Unconventional, top-quality programme. A must for film freaks! *St-Jakobs-Platz 1; Tel. 23 32 41 50; S- and U-Bahn: Marienplatz*

Forum der Technik [118 C4]
Part of the Deutsches Museum. The first Imax cinema in Germany. Unique documentary film centre with the most famous natural history films in special sound quality. An impressive experience for young and old. *Museumsinsel 1; Tel. 21 12 51 80; S-Bahn: Isartor*

Maxx [111 F5]

Ultra-modern cinema in super-ugly building. Extra comfy seats, state-of-the-art technology and own diner. Mostly box-office hits only. *Isartorplatz 9; Beware of the telephone rip-off: Tel. 01805-24 63 62 99 (12 Cent/min.), 50 Cent per ticket reservation! S-Bahn: Isartor*

Multiplex [110 A3]

Munich's largest multiplex cinema is currently under construction between Bayerstrasse and Schlosserstrasse, on the site of the former giant Mathäser cinema. Due to open in 2003, and boasting 4,500 seats, it is likely to make life more difficult for the art cinema owners. *Bayerstrasse 3; S- and U-Bahn: Stachus*

Münchner Filmpassage [111 F5]

Best video rental in town. Almost all films are in the original language – a goldmine for film freaks. Very helpful staff. *Daily, except Sun (not included in the price) 9 am–midnight; Tel. 29 62 17; Zweibrückenstrasse 8; S-Bahn: Isartor*

Museumslichtspiele [118 C4]

Sophisticated cinematic art in four auditoria at the Deutsches Museum: they've been showing the 'Rocky Horror Picture Show' here since time immemorial! Also English-language films. *Lilienstrasse 2/ Ludwigsbrücke; Tel. 48 24 03; S-Bahn: Isartor or Rosenheimer Platz; tram: 18*

Insider Tip
Neues Rottmanns [118 A1]

Art-house cinema with top-level repertoire. Lone campaigner against the Mafia-like film distributors and multiplex owners. Rated highly among genuine film buffs. *Rott-*

mannstrasse 15; Tel. 52 16 83; U-Bahn: 1, Stiglmaierplatz*

Filmtheater Sendlinger Tor [110 B5]

Munich's oldest cinema with old-fashioned charm. Big building, big screen. Run-of-the-mill food fodder. Box seats! *Sendlinger-Tor-Platz; Tel. 55 46 36; U-Bahn: 1/2/3/6, Sendlinger Tor*

Werkstattkino [110 C6]

Hard & Heavy, underground cinema with controversial, much-discussed material. B-movie temple and cult-status sex films. *Fraunhoferstrasse 9; Tel. 260 72 50; U-Bahn: 1/2, Fraunhoferstrasse*

PUBS

Atzinger [114 B6]

🏃 The ultimate student pub. Proximity to the university attracts high-IQ, early-morning tipplers. Terribly laid back. *Daily 10 am–3 am; Schellingstrasse 9; U-Bahn: 3/6, Universität*

Baader Café [118 B4]

The young clientele of old has aged along with the café, but it's still very much on the scene. Popular with local journalists. Music between soft rock and ambient. *Sun–Fri 10 am–1 am, Sat 10 am–2 am; Baaderstrasse 46; U-Bahn: 1/2, Fraunhoferstrasse*

Forum [118 B3]

One of those typical Munich pubs which changes its character according to the time of day. Super breakfast, pleasant lunch and almost student-bistro atmosphere in the evenings. In the summer you can sit outside. Chaotic, but likeable. *Sun–Thurs 8 am–1 am, Fri&Sat 8 am–3 am; Corneliusstrasse 2; tram: 17/18*

Nachtkantine [119 E4–5]

insider tip

Munich's craziest bar, at Kunstpark Ost. Meeting place of the never-tired and always-hungry – great if you can't sleep. *Sun–Thurs 10 am to 4 am, Fri 10 am–6 am, Sat noon to 6 am; Grafinger Strasse 6; S-Bahn: Ostbahnhof*

Café Puck [118 B1]

In true lemming fashion, everyone gravitates over here, because they can't stand the Roxy any longer. Breakfast until 6 pm, after that there's no escape! *Daily 9 am–1 am; Türkenstrasse 33; U-Bahn: 3/6, Universität*

Schmalznudel [111 D5]

Hot tip for breakfast before turning in, especially during Carnival. A favourite Munich classic on the Viktualienmarkt – all year round. *Mon–Sat 5 am–5 pm; Prälat-Zistl-Strasse 8; S- and U-Bahn: Marienplatz*

Valentinstüberl [117 F5]

Typical Munich! A tiny stand-up bar is taken over by a few young landlords, and within weeks has gone from a Bavarian-style tavern to a 'lounge', where 'live and let live' is the order of the day. Interesting seating! *Daily 6 pm–1 am; Dreimühlenstrasse 28; bus: 38, Ehrengutstrasse*

Ysenegger [113 D5]

Cosy and friendly Neuhausen bistro-pub with bearable noise level, excellent service and fair prices.

Daily 10 am–1 am; Ysenburger-strasse 3; U-Bahn: 1, Rotkreuzplatz

Zoozie'z [118 A5]

🏃 Yuppies' favourite brunch, i. e. an enormous spread of delicacies. Usually packed to the gills. The prices match the chic clientele to a T. *Sun–Wed 9 am–1 am, Thurs–Sat 9 am–3 am; Wittelsbacherstrasse 15; U-Bahn: 3/6, Goetheplatz; bus: 58*

Café Zweistein [118 B4]

★ Small, but impressive theatre buffet-bar with delicious food and extremely pleasant fellow guests – and all in Munich's nicest street. *Daily 9 am–1 am; Hans-Sachs-Strasse 12; U-Bahn: 1/2/3/6, Sendlinger Tor*

CONCERTS & OPERA

Gasteig [119 D4]

Munich has three world-class orchestras, the Munich Philharmonic Orchestra, the Bavarian State Opera and the Bavarian Broadcasting Corporation Symphony Orchestra. The Philharmonic, currently led by James Levine, is based at the Gasteig Culture Centre, the much-criticised 'culture-bunker' above the Isar. The main auditorium may be attractive to look at, but it has far from perfect acoustics. *Rosenheimer Strasse 5; tickets: Tel. 54 81 81 81; S-Bahn: Rosenheimer Platz*

Herkulessaal [111 E2]

Classical music in a Classicist setting: the Hercules Hall in the Residenz is the mecca of Munich's concert-goers. *Residenzstrasse 1 (entr. Hofgartenstrasse); Tel. 29 06 71; U-Bahn: 3/4/5/6, Odeonsplatz*

Musikhochschule [110 B1]

Recommended for lovers of so-called 'serious' music. Concerts often feature young guest artists from the master classes of Europe's music academies. *Arcisstrasse 1; Tel. 28 92 74 40; U-Bahn: 2, Königsplatz*

Nationaltheater [111 E3]

Munich's No. 1 opera house, and No. 1 in the state subsidies charts, too. *Max-Joseph-Platz; Tel. 21 85 19 20; U-Bahn: 3/4/5/6, Odeonsplatz; tram: 19*

Prinzregententheater [119 E2]

Grandiose reconstruction of the former Opera House. Today, chiefly used as a concert hall, it prides itself on its excellent acoustics – the best

Munich's opera: the Nationaltheater on Max-Joseph-Platz

in town – and its wonderful café. *Prinzregentenplatz 12; Tel. 21 85 02; U-Bahn: 4, Prinzregentenplatz*

Staatstheater am Gärtnerplatz [111 D6]

Prestigious address, wrongly dubbed a mere subsidiary of the Opera. *Gärtnerplatz 3; Tel. 201 67 67; U-Bahn: 1/2, Fraunhoferstrasse*

CULTURAL CENTRES

Pasinger Fabrik [0] *Inside Tip*

To understand the phenomenon 'Pasinger Fabrik', you have to know a bit about the character of the district. Incorporated into the greater Munich area in 1933, the residents still look on themselves as 'Pasinger' and not as 'Münchner'. So it is perhaps unusual that one of the most ambitious cultural projects in the city should be launched in Pasing of all places. In the old factory building directly to the north of the railway station, exhibitions, drama and concerts of all kinds take place; even Munich's smallest opera house is based here (once you've seen Mozart's *The Abduction from the Seraglio* here, you won't want to go to a state theatre again). There is a children's and young people's cultural workshop, a youth forum, an adult education centre and the 'Rote Rüben' (Red Carrots) theatre – the classic repertoire of a city controlled by Social Democrats. Focal point is the café-restaurant, run by Cantina GmbH (plc), which is also in charge of Ruffini. There's a classic brunch every Sunday and a choice selection of wines. The gallery shows changing exhibitions. And what's more, the S-Bahn back to Munich departs right in front of your nose! *Tues–Sun 11 am–10.30 pm; August-Exter-Strasse 1; Tel. 82 92 90 79; www.pasinger-fabrik. com; S-Bahn: Pasing*

CLUBS

Atomic Café [111 F4]

Not far from the Opera and Dallmayr's, party to the sound of today's youth. Pop music for people for whom hip-hop and Hamburger Schule is about as serious as life gets. Tomorrow's trends, today. *Sun, Tues–Thurs 9.59 pm–3 am; Fri&Sat 9.59 pm–4 am; Neuturmstrasse 5; Tel. 228 30 54; U-Bahn: 3/6, Marienplatz*

Always good for a laugh: the Münchner Lustspielhaus and its top-notch cabaret

Feierwerk [117 D4]

Locally-subsidised, permanent up-and-coming rock star festival. Cheap tickets and a feast for the ears, time and time again. *Programme: daily 9 pm–1 am; Hansastrasse 39; Tel. 769 36 00; S- and U-Bahn: Heimeranplatz*

Jazzclub Unterfahrt [119 E3]

For a reasonable admission charge, jazz fans can experience the – still – high-class Munich jazz scene plus big international stars. The Sunday evening jam sessions are the real highlight. *Sun–Thurs 6 pm–1 am, Fri&Sat 6 pm–3 am; Einsteinstrasse 42; tickets and programme: Tel. 448 27 94; U-Bahn: 4/5, Max-Weber-Platz*

ᴵⁿˢⁱᵈᵉʳ Muffathalle [118 C3]

★ Concerts, dance, drama, performance. Two Green politicians snapped up a real bargain here. Subsidised sub-culture, a great café and in summer a romantic beer garden – a bonus for the city. *Daily 6 pm–4 am; Zellstrasse 4; Tel. 45 87 50 00; S-Bahn: Rosenheimer Platz or Isartor*

Münchner Lustspielhaus [115 D4] ᴵⁿˢⁱᵈᵉʳ Tip

Superlative small-stage artistry in plush surroundings, from singer-songwriters to cabaret to concerts. *Daily 6 pm–1 am; Occamstrasse 8; Tel. 34 49 74; U-Bahn: 3/6, Münchner Freiheit*

New Backstage [116 A1]

Munich's main crossover pub. Independent music: loud, young, freaky. Just been transplanted to the northern end of Friedenheim Bridge. *Daily 7 pm–1 am; Wilhelm-Hale-Strasse/Birkenweg; Tel. 126 61 00; www.backstage.de; S-Bahn: Friedenheimerbrücke*

Night Club im Bayerischen Hof [111 D3]

Munich's most prestigious jazz venue. International greats from Doldinger to Zawinul make guest appearances. Elsewhere in town, jazz clubs are closing down; here, they're still going strong, with a little help from the hotel profits to fall back on. The drinks may be expensive, but the music is a good investment any time. *Promenadeplatz 2–6; Tel. 212 09 94; S- and U-Bahn: Stachus*

Podium [114 B4]

This corner building tucked away to the right of Leopoldstrasse was originally dedicated solely to Dixieland, with frenzied, nebulous morning sessions. Today, it's the haunt of the *crème de la crème* of Munich's rock musicians, indulging their love of cover versions. When 'The Public' are playing, you'll hear a convincing rendition of *Satisfaction*, and believe Jim Morrison has risen from the dead. *Sun–Thurs 8 pm–1 am, Fri&Sat 8 pm–3 am; Wagnerstrasse 1; Tel. 39 94 82; U-Bahn: 3/6, Münchner Freiheit*

Wirtshaus im Schlachthof [117 F5]

★ Where livestock dealers used to devour their *Weisswurst* at 6 o'clock in the morning, heavy rock music blasts out every evening. The wonderful wood-panelled hall of this traditional tavern is one of the most popular venues for those bands who wouldn't quite fill the Olympic Hall. Up to 500 fans let their hair down and, when the heat is on, cool down in the beer garden. Mixed musical bag, plus plenty of satirical and political cabaret, the latter regularly showcased live on television. *Mon–Thurs 11 am–1 am, Fri 11 am–3 am, Sat 5 pm–3 am, Sun 5 pm–1 am; Zenettistrasse 9; Tel. 76 54 84; U-Bahn: 3/6, Goetheplatz; bus: 38, Zenettistrasse*

Altes Residenztheater (Cuvilliés-Theater) [111 E3]

Architectural jewel, and home to the Staatsschauspiel theatre company. Occasional chamber music concerts. *Max-Joseph-Platz 1; Tel. 21 85 19 20; U-Bahn: 3/6, Odeonsplatz*

Deutsches Theater [118 A3]

Everything from Carnival ball to operetta to singer-songwriter concerts. *Schwanthalerstrasse 13; Tel. 55 23 44 44; S- and U-Bahn: Stachus*

i-camp [118 B5]

Formerly the 'Neues Theater' (New Theatre) and true to its name, it is now even more way-out, more experimental and more inclined to incorporate new media into its productions. *Entenbachstrasse 37; Tel. 65 00 00; U-Bahn: 1/2, Kolumbusplatz*

Komödie im Bayerischen Hof [111 D3]

Boulevard theatre for people who like dressing up. *Promenadeplatz/Prannerstrasse; Tel. 29 28 10; S- and U-Bahn: Stachus or Marienplatz*

Marionettentheater [110 C6]

Traditional theatre under new management. For music-loving children, they give a wonderful performance of the *Magic Flute*. *Blumenstrasse 29a; Tel. 26 57 12; U-Bahn: 1/2/3/6, Sendlinger Tor*

Metropol [0]

New theatre with bags of energy and courage; they even play *Black Rider* by Robert Wilson. Or The Bible – in two hours. *Florians-*

*mühlstrasse 5; Tel. 32 19 55 33;
U-Bahn: 6, Freimann*

Münchner Kammerspiele
(Schauspielhaus)   [111 F3–4]
Managed by Dieter Dorn for many years, the Kammerspiele progressed to become Munich's leading drama theatre, famous for its wide repertoire, ranging from classical Greek to premieres of contemporary plays. Frank Baumbauer has taken over from Dorn.

The theatre is currently undergoing extremely costly renovation; performances take place in the rehearsal rooms at *Maximilianstrasse 26; Tel. 23 33 70 00; U-Bahn: 3/6, Odeonsplatz or Marienplatz*, or alternatively at *Dachauer Strasse 114; tram: 12.*

Pathos Transport   [113 E5]
Workshop for new German plays. Excellent reputation. *Dachauer Strasse 110; Tel. 12 73 97 09; bus: 33*

Residenztheater   [111 E3]
Bavarian State Theatre Company, heavily subsidised and still a favourite grindstone on which critics like to grind their axes. Dieter Dorn is now at the helm here. It remains to be seen whether he can steer the theatre away from its reputation for mediocrity, and culture a few pearls. *Max-Joseph-Platz 1; Tel. 21 85 19 40; U-Bahn: 3/4/5/6, Odeonsplatz; tram: 19*

Schauburg   [114 B5]
Municipal theatre for young people. Under competent management, a most promising company. Worth a try! *Franz-Joseph-Strasse 47; Tel. 23 33 71 71; U-Bahn: 2, Hohenzollernplatz; tram: 18*

TamS – Theater
am Sozialamt   [115 D4]
One of the oldest private theatres in the city, recognised avant-garde and modern programme. In the finest Schwabing tradition. Titled 'Welthinterhoftheater' (World Backyard Theatre) by the *Süddeutsche Zeitung. Haimhauserstrasse 13a; Tel. 34 58 90; U-Bahn: 3/6, Münchner Freiheit*

Theater Blaue Maus   [113 E6]
Dare to put on Brecht, though not always a success. *Elvirastrasse 17a; Tel. 18 26 94; U-Bahn: 1, Maillingerstrasse –*

Theater und ... so fort   [118 B4]
New name, new manager: now produces a wild, exciting mixture of amateur dramatics and dramatic art ... and so forth. Adventure for theatre freaks. Bar for emergencies (10 am–9 pm) in the foyer. Matinées, too. *Hans-Sachs-Strasse 12; Tel. 23 21 98 77; U-Bahn: Sendlinger Tor*

Theater 44   [114 C4]
Old, private theatre. Variable quality. *Hohenzollernstrasse 20; Tel. 322 87 48; U-Bahn: 3/6, Münchner Freiheit*

Volkstheater   [118 A1]
Oscillates between comedy and quality. In 2002, highly acclaimed, theatrical *grande dame* Ruth Drexel was succeeded as theatre manager by Christian Stückl, who after all directed the last, critically-acclaimed Oberammergau *Passionsspiele* (Passion Play) and Hauptmann's *Jedermann* in Salzburg in 2002. *Brienner Strasse 50; Tel. 523 46 55; U-Bahn: 1, Stiglmaierplatz*

Munich at random

**These walking tours are marked in green
on the map on the back cover and in the Street Atlas
beginning on page 110**

1 BARGAIN-HUNTING

**For this walk, you can
safely leave your credit
card at home. All you
need on this bargain-
hunt is a bit of cash, lots of time
and to feel like chatting – for the
best part of an afternoon.**

All you really need is what
Bavarians call a 'Leiterwagerl', a
little wooden handcart to pull along
behind you – to transport your
accumulated treasures in! Begin
your walk with breakfast at the
Friesische Teestube (p. 53) on nostalgic Pündtplatz. Thus strength-
ened, just a few hundred metres to
the west in Belgradstrasse, at No.
19, you'll find *Muskelkater*, where
you can buy all manner of second-
hand sports equipment – the shop
is named after the aching muscles
you get after working out!

If you're into fashion, then go
along to *Pat's Boutique* at nearby
Hohenzollernstrasse 44 and look
out for a little something by Armani
or Versace *(Pat's Boutique* is also at
Dachauer Strasse 20 and *Sonnen-
strasse 2)*. Our route takes you on
into the heart of Schwabing, to

*The Hofbräuhaus: your destination
on the third walking tour*

Haimhauserstrasse 6 and *Karola's
Exklusiv Secondhandshop*.

If by now you are in need of a
bite to eat, then pop into the *Café
Münchner Freiheit*; the cakes taste
marvellous.

Take the U-Bahn (there's still
quite a bit of walking to do) into the
city centre. Get off at Marienplatz
and resist the temptation to go into
Beck's department store. Instead,
walk over to *Shirokko* at Ledererstrasse 19, where you'll find music
from all over the world – an audio
trip round the globe. Regardless of
whether you've found something
suitable, move on to *Böhmler* in Tal.
It may be one of the most expensive
furnishing shops in town, but at the
rear of the arcade of the same
name, you can often find fabulous
special offers. Who knows, maybe
you can get them to deliver?

On the other side of Tal, you
come to the *Viktualienmarkt (p. 68)*,
which has a reputation for being
particularly expensive. This is not
absolutely true. It is possible to buy
a pretzel for just 50 Cent, asparagus
prices differ by up to 100 per cent,
and at the wine bars it is essential to
inquire about special offers.

This area is not only the most
typical of Munich, it also has the
largest number of classy bargain
shops. Here are just a few: right

Insider Tip

next to the Viktualienmarkt begins Reichenbachstrasse. On the corner with Frauenstrasse is *Samen Dehner*, a Garden of Eden for horticulture fans. Round the corner at Rumfordstrasse 30 is Munich's most colourful hammock shop. Via Müllerstrasse, make your way to Fraunhoferstrasse, turn left as far as the *restaurant (p. 59)* of the same name. At No. 1 is *Margit Muggenthalers Trödelladen (p. 67)*, the most charming junk shop in town with the most charming junk collector running it.

Back to Müllerstrasse, this time to the left. A veritable paradise for passionate browsers: *Spiel Art* (opposite the Hypovereinsbank) is ideal for all men who are really boys at heart, and at *Birdies Nest*, on the corner of Holzstrasse and Pestalozzistrasse, jazz fans can immerse themselves in the past. Now it's time to take stock over a beer and a snack. We recommend the *Faun (Westermühlstrasse, on the corner with Hans-Sachs-Strasse)*, where the menu ranges from chilli to *Schweinsbraten*, and you can choose to sit outside while you work out how much damage you've done to your purse or wallet!

2 ARCHITECTURAL TOUR ON WHEELS

Munich is more than Frauenkirche and Maximilianeum. The last 30 years have given rise to some pioneering architecture, scattered all over the city – which is why this 'walk' is on wheels, whether two or eight. Duration: no matter how fit you are, give yourself at least four hours.

Munich – Capital of modern architecture, would be an alternative

Antiquitäten Muggenthaler hoards treasures of times past

name for this tour. To enable you to reach the individual subjects of interest in a suitably up-to-date way, we have chosen a route which is ideal for skating or cycling. Inline skates can be hired for approximately 8 Euro per day (including protective gear), for example at *Sporthaus Schuster (Rosenstrasse 1–5; Tel. 23 70 70; U-Bahn: Marienplatz)*. Those of you who are not so comfortable on skates can hire a bicycle at the railway station (see 'Practical Information').

Take the U-Bahn to the *Olympiagelände (p. 30)*, an ideal opportunity to 'run in' your skates and soak up the wonderful atmosphere. The 70,000-seat stadium was built by Germany's leading architect Günter Behnisch for the 'friendly Games' of 1972 (which then ended so tragically with the PLO terrorist attack). Its stunning, innovative roof construction is still unique in the world, and the stadium has managed what others seldom do, namely to become a symbol of a whole city.

Leave the Olympic Park, past the ice arena, going east and glide over the bridge across the central ring road. The world's biggest four-leaf clover awaits you: the *BMW-Hochhaus* (office block). Arranged like four engine cylinders, the motor giant's headquarters is a milestone of high-tech architecture, built in 1972 to a design by Karl Schwanzer.

Right, take a deep breath, here comes a longer, but very attractive stretch. Via Milbertshofenerstrasse, continue to the North Cemetery. The *English Garden* begins here, which you skirt, along Osterwaldstrasse. Cross the ring road again (there's a convenient parapet for the unsteady) and take a well-earned rest in the Osterwaldgarten. Continue via Kieferstrasse and Mandlstrasse in the prettiest part of Schwabing to Tivolistrasse, on which you cross the English Garden to the *Tucherpark*. Here you'll find what was classed, in the 1970s, as an architectural sensation: the *Bayerische Rückversicherung* building (Bavarian Reinsurance Company). With this structure, Uwe Kiessler laid the foundations of his worldwide reputation as a truly innovative architect.

The paths of skater and cyclist part here, due to the hill to be negotiated. While the skaters treat themselves to a beer at the *Chinese Tower*, the cyclists embark on a bonus detour, pedalling along Montgelasstrasse as far as Effnerplatz to marvel at the *Hypohochhaus (p. 20)*. It looks like it would be more at home in Chicago, and was designed at the end of the 1980s by Walter and Bea Betz as a grand affirmation of capitalism. Doubling back the way they came, across the Max-Joseph Bridge again and, watching out for pedestrians, the skaters roll along the pavement of Emil-Riedl-Strasse as far as Prinzregentenstrasse, then to the corner of Bruderstrasse, where Otto Seidler's latest creation stands, a gigantic residential and office complex, a riot of colour from strident blue to British racing green.

Reunited once again at Türkenstrasse 30 (the skaters arriving via Von-der-Tannstrasse and Theresienstrasse). This is the site of Munich's *Architekturgalerie* (Architecture Gallery) showing the latest designs. Don't forget to take your skates off!

A walk through 'text-book' Munich holds surprises, if you are willing to give yourself up to the niceties of the Bavarian lifestyle. Depending on refreshment breaks, the tour takes around three hours.

No trip to Munich is complete without it; you really must take a look at 'classic' Munich, the way it is depicted in the media everywhere. The city of pealing bells and creaking *Lederhosen*! You don't

The Frauenkirche is the starting point of this classic Bavarian walking tour

necessarily have to buy a traditional *Gamsbarthut* to wear on your walk – not that it would do any harm. Just remember to take it off again right at the start, since the tour begins at the *Frauenkirche (p. 25)*.

Overwhelmed by the severity of the late-Gothic architecture and the ride up the south tower (99 metres), stroll eastwards to Marienplatz, possibly just in time for the 11 o'clock Glockenspiel spectacle. You have earned a rest by now; try the *Weisses Bräuhaus (p. 61)*. Be careful, though; it's still early and the beer is strong, the day ahead is long and the next temptation just around the corner. At the *Valentin-Karlstadt-Musäum (p. 47)* at the end of Tal in the Isartor, you can enjoy *Weisswurst* and a *Weissbier* to wash it down.

Like any self-respecting Bavarian, you too are drawn towards the *Maximilianeum*, seat of the State Parliament *(p. 20)*. Take Thierschstrasse, which runs from Zweibrückenstrasse to Maximilianstrasse, and indulge in the odd spontaneous detour, say, along Adelgundenstrasse. Here you'll find examples of Munich town house architecture, the like of which was all but destroyed in other cities during World War II.

Just time for a glance at the State Parliament, then turn left into Maximilianstrasse, past the Upper Bavarian administration building, heading west towards Max-Joseph-Platz.

Shake your head, in the manner of all the other wearers of *Gamsbarthüte,* over the cheeky kids hurtling around on their inline skates in front of the venerable *Nationaltheater (p. 21)* and drown

Danger: modern art! 'Walking Man' in Leopoldstrasse

your sorrows over 'the youth of today' with a glass of No. 4 a at the *Pfälzer Weinprobierstuben* in the Residenz.

Ludwigstrasse, that austere boulevard, lies before you. Passing the *Geschwister-Scholl-Institut*, the *Staatsbibliothek* (State Library) and the *Ludwig-Maximilians-Universität (p. 24)*, turn right at the Victory Gate into narrow Ohmstrasse, before eye-strain sets in at the sight of the huge *Walking Man* (Danger: modern art!) in Leopoldstrasse. It's better to stroll down Königinstrasse towards the city centre, or one of the paths running parallel to it through the English Garden, to then approach the *Haus der Kunst (p. 43)* from behind. Overshadowed perhaps by its inglorious past, the gallery's marriage of exhibition rooms and theatre – realised due to the freeing-up of space when the

Modern Art Gallery moved out – is a truly up-to-the-minute concept.

If that was all too tiring, wander through Lehel (Liebigstrasse) up to Widenmayerstrasse and across to the Praterinsel. At the *Alpine Museum (p. 40)* you can find out where the tuft of hair on top of your *Gamsbarthut* comes from, or carry on past the Muffathalle (non-*Gamsbarthut*-wearers only!) to the *Müllersches Volksbad (p. 21)*. There's always time for a steam bath, and you can borrow everything you need.

Last stop: *Hofbräuhaus (p. 60)*. 'Kellnerin, a Mass!' is the standard phrase here, which is the polite way of asking the waitress for a litre of beer. The atmosphere at *Dürnbräu* in the street of the same name, however, is more authentic and typical of Munich. What better way to toast the success of your Munich trip? *Zum Wohl!*

A little piece of heaven

Pleasure-loving monks, sparkling white boats, Baroque towns and cosy taverns await the day-tripper from Munich

1 ON YOUR BIKE ROUND LAKE STARNBERG

The secretive landscape between Starnberger See and Ammersee is actually best explored on foot. On the saddle of a bicycle, though, you can get a better feel for the region's stories, stories which are so full of goblins, fairies and friendly ghosts that they inspired some of the fantastic tales by author Michael Ende. His delightful account of the good ghost Gogolori is based on one such old legend. Allow around five hours cycling time for the 75-km tour – and don't forget your swimming trunks or bikini!

The keener cyclists among you can take the S-Bahn S 6 only as far as *Mühltal*. Here you'll find one of the most attractive beer gardens to the south of Munich, with Dixieland music at the weekends *(Wirtshaus Obermühltal; Tues–Sun noon*

Cycling round the Starnberger See entitles you to a rest and a swim to recover

to midnight; beer garden open from 10 am; Tel. 08151-85 85).

Then it's 'on yer bike' down into the Würm valley **[122 B3]** and off towards Starnberg! Those few kilometres are ideal as a warm-up.

You can safely give *Starnberg* **[122 B4]** a miss. The town may be one of the richest in Bavaria, but it is also one of the ugliest. So, head down and off to Weilheim. Turn right at the traffic lights on the hill towards Söcking. To the left of the road, a well-maintained cycle path leads a hilly 14 kilometres to *Andechs* **[122 A–B4]**, a name which makes beer lovers and monastery experts sit up and take notice. Its Benedictine monastery is where, instead of dedicating themselves to teaching, the monks turned to the noble art of brewing. Other specialities include Andechs cheese and *Obatzda (Klostergasthof: daily 10 am–midnight; warm meals: 11 am to 10 pm; Bergstrasse 16; Tel. 08152-9 30 90; €).*

Such is the curse over this sacred mountain, that it is easier to come up it than to come down again. So the cyclist drinks a less-alcoholic, so-called *Radler* ('cyclist' in German) and pedals on. To the south, the road forks. To the right, it leads to Herrsching on the Ammersee. Our tour turns left towards Machtlfing and Starnberg Lake. Those who forgot to 'fill up' at Andechs can do so in Machtlfing at the *Höfler-Wirt (Tel. 08157-17 27)* and treat themselves to the best *Leberkäse* in the area.

A beautiful, narrow, winding and little-used road leads to the primary route B 2, which you follow for around a hundred metres southwards. Soon the road takes you down across green pastures to Garatshausen and *Tutzing* **[122 B4]**. Time for a swim!

The water in the *Tutzinger Bucht* (Tutzing Bay) is calm and clean, especially when the prevailing west wind is blowing. There are sailing boats for hire and, since you don't need a licence in Bavaria, anyone who knows the difference between windward and leeward can hire one *(approx. 10 Euro per hour, according to type and size).*

But this is a cycle tour after all, so back in the saddle and on south along the beautiful cycle path towards *Bernried*, with yet another harbour lined with hundreds of boats. The marina here is the only one without a sailing club, but it does have moorings for use by guests of the Marina Hotel *(Hotel Marina, Am Yachthafen 1–15; Tel. 08158-93 20; €€).*

A few kilometres further on is the new *Buchheim Museum*, a must for art lovers. The building houses a wide range of collections, most notably of Expressionist works, including many by the artists' group 'Die Brücke', and is a real crowd-puller. *(Buchheim Collection – Museum of Fantasy; Tues*

Insider Tip

to Fri 10 am–5 pm, Sat&Sun 10 am to 6 pm; Am Hirschgarten 1).

Carry on as far as Seeseiten. The restaurant owned by fisher Dommaschk is in such a pretty location, you won't mind the chance to get your breath back while you are waiting for the waitress. To try one of the home-made cakes or freshly-caught fish is to know what it means to be in Bavaria. *(Café Seeseiten; daily 9 am–7 pm; warm meals: 11.30 am–2.30 pm only; Tel. 08801-7 42; €).*

Insider Tip

It's not far now to the southern end of Lake Starnberg and the little town of *Seeshaupt* **[122 B4]**. Here at the lido is a pretty bathing beach and pleasant beer garden *(lido: daily 9 am–midnight; warm meals: 11 am to 11 pm; Sankt-Heinrich-Strasse 113; Tel. 08801-533).*

From here you continue along the eastern side of the lake as far as *Münsing* **[122 B4]**. If you wish, you can go at a leisurely pace to Starnberg, or if stamina and enthusiasm haven't yet deserted you, make a tricky detour. In Münsing turn right towards Wolfratshausen. Leaving the village, turn left towards Dorfen, along a tiny road with no other traffic through woods and meadows. After the motorway underpass, ride past a farm with a fabulous view across the Isar valley. In Dorfen turn right then left onto the B 11 as far as Ebenhausen. There, you turn right and take the hair-raising route downhill to Schäftlarn Monastery **[122 C4]**.

You are now on the 1972 Olympic cycling route, sweating as you head uphill along the eastern bank of the Isar, just like the heroes of yesteryear. Then finally, in Strasslach **[122 C3]**, a wonderful restaur-

Stopping off in Andechs for its famous beer is a must

ant awaits you: *Gasthof zum Wild-park (daily 9.30 am–midnight; warm meals: 11.30 am–9.30 pm; Tölzer Strasse 2; Tel. 08170-635; €€)*; also a very good idea for an evening culinary trip.

From here it's just a short ride back to Munich – without any hills to torture those poor muscles. If even that seems too much, you can take the tram from Grünwald.

2 OFF TO LOWER BAVARIA

In Munich, if someone admits to coming from Lower Bavaria, they are greeted with a pitying smile – such are the subtleties of the inner-Bavarian pecking order. A day trip of approximately 250 km – allow yourself four hours driving time – is an excursion to the non-tourist-oriented part of Bavaria, into its heartland where an independent people speak their own particular dialect, where gently rolling hills predominate and immensely rich farmers rule the roost like the rural landowners of old. The tour takes you via Landshut, Vilsbiburg, Altötting and back to Munich.

Our route takes you via the motorway in the direction of Nuremberg, as far as the intersection at Neufahrn **[122 C2]**, where you turn right towards Deggendorf and Munich airport. Continue on the motorway to exit Moosburg-Nord **[123 D1]**. From here, follow the B 11 to *Landshut* **[123 E1]**.

From a distance you can already see the tiled roof of the 130.6-m-high tower (the second-highest of its kind in the world) of the wonderful, Gothic St Martin's Cathedral on the eastern edge of the old part of town.

Landshut is an idyllic place: rich, solid middle-class, an architectural wonderland. The recurrent celebration of the Royal Wedding is a world-famous attraction. Beyond that, however, Landshut, with its magnificent Trausnitz Castle, is rated as one of the most beautiful towns in Bavaria.

Take time to stroll through the arcades in the old part of town and window-shop in the small galleries. Don't neglect the new town (which is quite old, too), or forget to have a break at one of the street cafés. The food at *Koch-Wirt (daily 9 am–1 am; warm meals: 9 am–11 pm; Altstadt 388; Tel. 0871-222 24; €)* is good homely fare. Alternatively, the *Weickmannshöhe* on the Hofberg offers a superb view of the countryside *(daily 11 am–2.30 pm, 3.30 pm to midnight; warm meals: until 11 pm; Weickmannshöhe 13; Tel. 0871-241 18; €€)*. Beforehand you must take a look at the Town Hall and Trausnitz Castle *(Oct–Mar: daily 9 am–noon, 1 pm–4 pm; Apr–Sept: 1 pm–5 pm)*, plus the *Burgcafé (Tel. 0871-263 31)!*

Two kilometres outside town, you reach the B 299 to *Vilsbiburg* **[123 E1]**. The old town gateway and the townscape down to the River Vils are quite pretty, with just the odd architectural *faux pas* here and there. The parish church is typical of the region, in that it is modelled on St Martin's in Landshut. On the hill to the east stands the pilgrimage church Mariä Hilf. You don't need to go that far, since you turn right towards Velden before you come to the old part of Vilsbiburg. Off into the sticks!

Follow the valley to the left upstream along the Vils, through little hamlets like Frauenhaarbach or Vilslern (lots of atmospheric pubs round about) as far as Velden. Drive straight through to Buchbach and on to Schwindegg. This is no race track, but a route to be savoured. You're in the prettiest part of Lower Bavaria, with not a tourist in sight (honestly!), and you'd be hard put to find a stretch of road which is as romantic as that from Schwindegg to Mühldorf **[123 F2]**.

Mühldorf itself is no great shakes. *Altötting* **[123 F2]** is. Not only because of the Chapel of Grace, but also because at the *Hotel zur Post (restaurant: daily 7 am–10 pm; Kapellplatz 2; Tel. 08671-50 40; €€)*, you are the guest of a former top Bavarian politician who once greased a few palms too many. But that's another story.

If you were late leaving Munich, you had better be heading back home on the B 12. Be careful, though, as this is one of the most dangerous stretches of road in Bavaria, and justifiably has many concealed speed traps.

If there's still time to spare, you could take another route back, if you don't mind a 60-km detour. Stop off at *Burghausen* **[123 F3]**, just 17 kilometres away, and drop in for a meal at the *Hotel Post (daily 6.30 am–1 am; Am Stadtplatz 39; Tel. 08677-96 50; €€)*. A visit to the castle is also a must *(the castle is always open; guided tours: Tel. 08677-24 35)*.

Finally, you head slightly southwest via Trostberg and Altenmarkt, then westwards in the direction of *Wasserburg* [123 E3]. It's time for a little rest!

The old part of town is beautiful and compensates a little for the slightly boring remaining journey back to Munich. Southwest of Ebersberg [123 D3], near Glonn, [123 D4] is *Herrmannsdorf*, site of the Herrmannsdorf ecological agricultural workshops and the affili-ated restaurant, *Schweinsbräu (closed Mon and Tues; Tel. 08093-90 94 45; €€)*. The *Süddeutsche Zeitung* once commented, 'You can taste that they farm happy pigs here!' From here, the tour takes you back to Munich via Glonn and Siegertsbrunn.

Insider Tip

3 A BOAT TRIP ON THE CHIEMSEE

40 km; duration: 2 1/2 hours incl. long tour, 1 hour incl. short tour

You could begin by taking the motorway past Rosenheim as far as the Bernau exit (No. 106) [123 E4]. Take a boat trip right round the Chiemsee. (If you've time to spare, you could cross over to the Herreninsel and take a look at Ludwig II's palace). Head back via Bernau, Marquartstein, Reit im Winkl, Kössen, Walchsee and Oberaudorf, back onto the Kufstein–Rosenheim motorway and on to Munich. *Chiemsee Steamer Fleet in Prien; Tel. 08051-60 90*

The Fama-Brunnen in Herrenchiemsee: one stop on your Chiemsee tour

Absolutely in!

Essential events, meetings and happenings you can't afford to miss

Blade Night – on eight wheels through the city

Eighteen times a year, the skating fraternity meets towards evening in Sophienstrasse, to skate some 15 kilometres through the city. The routes are conceived to avoid slopes and poor, unsuitable road surfaces. Since the whole project depends on the weather, you should find out beforehand whether and when the whole

thing is getting off the ground. Either under *www.muenchner-blade-night.de* or send an SMS with the text 'Blade In' to *Tel. 0179-501 76 52* to get information directly via your mobile phone. *Sophienstrasse; S- and U-Bahn: Stachus*

Boules

From spring till late in the autumn, the pavements between Odeonsplatz and the state chancellery are a giant playground for *boules* freaks. Weather permitting, you can often hear the metallic clicking sound until sunset or later. *Hofgarten; U-Bahn: 3/6, Odeonsplatz*

Poetry Slam

At *Substanz*, a fairly freaky music venue, the young literati of Munich meet every *second Sunday in the month at 8 pm* for a poetry slam session. Entitled 'Speak & Spin', this is a reading competition in which the audience decides by acclamation on winners and losers. *Information by e-mail under munichslam@yahoo.de. Substanz; Ruppertstrasse 28; U-Bahn: 3/6, Pocchistrasse*

Salsa

Salsa fans can dance somewhere different almost every day: *Tues, from 9 pm: Hansa-Palast; Hansastrasse 41; Tel. 769 56 37; www.ritmo-latino.de; U-Bahn: 6, Partnachplatz; Sat and Wed, from 9 pm* (free dancing lessons: 9 pm–10 pm): *Max's; Maximilianstrasse 34; Tel. 22 80 17 00; U-Bahn: 3/6, Odeonsplatz or Marienplatz; Wed, from 8 pm: Max-Emanuel; Adalbertstrasse 33; Tel. 271 51 58; U-Bahn: 3/6, Universität; Thurs&Fri: Centro Habana* (free admission); *Isartalstrasse 26; bus: 31, from Sendlinger Tor to Ehrengutstrasse*

From Banks to Time Zones

Useful addresses and information for your trip to Munich

BANKS

Banking hours are Mon–Fri, 9 am–6 pm.

BICYCLE RENTAL

Radius Touristik
At main railway station opposite platforms 30–36; Tel. 59 61 13; May–Oct: daily 10 am–6 pm; 3 Euro per hour, 13 Euro per day

Call a Bike
Call a Bike has 2,000 bikes positioned at telephone boxes, (released by entering an electronic code). Simply return the bike to any telephone box. Payment is by credit card, basic price: 1 Euro, charged by the minute; one hour costs approx. 1 Euro. *Tel. 0800-522 55 22; www.callabike.de*

CUSTOMS

Travellers from other EU countries are no longer subject to customs checks. Visitors from other countries must observe the following limits, except for items for personal use. Duty free are: max. 50 g perfume, 200 cigarettes, 50 cigars, 250 g tobacco, 1 l of spirits (over 22% vol.), 2 l of spirits (under 22% vol.), 2 l of any wine. Gifts to the value of up to 175 Euro may be brought into Germany.

DRIVING

Drivers require a valid driving licence and vehicle documentation. It is advisable to carry an international green insurance card. Speed limits are as follows: highways: 130 km/h (80 mph) (recommended); overland: 80/100 km/h (50 mph/62 mph); built-up areas: 50 km/h (30 mph). The maximum level of alcohol in the blood is 0.5 mg/l. Seat belts are compulsory for all drivers and passengers.

EMBASSIES

UK
Bürkleinstrasse 10; Tel. 21 10 90; U-Bahn: 4/5, Lehel

USA
Königinstrasse 5; Tel. 288 80 or 288 87 22; U-Bahn: 4/5, S-Bahn: 3/6, Odeonsplatz

CANADA
Tal 29; Tel. 219 95 70; S-Bahn: 1/2/4/5/6/7/8, Isartor

EMERGENCIES

Police: *110;* Fire brigade and ambulance service: *112;* ADAC breakdown service: *0180-2 22 22 22;* Emergency medical service: *55 17 71;* Emergency dental service: *7 23 30 93;* 24-hr pharmacy: *59 44 75*

British nationals can claim any health service costs incurred in Germany on returning home. Be sure to apply for the E 111 form before leaving Britain. US and Canadian nationals should check with their health insurance company if they are covered for trips abroad and, if so, should carry proof of cover with them.

EURO

One Euro = 100 cents. Bank notes to the value of 5, 10, 20, 50, 100, 200 and 500 Euro and coins to the value of 1, 2, 5, 10, 20 and 50 cents and 1 and 2 Euro are in circulation.

GETTING TO MUNICH

By air

Munich can be reached direct from most European capitals, from a number of cities in the USA and from Canada via Frankfurt. The quickest way into the city is by S-Bahn (suburban train network): cost: 9 Euro. A bus links the airport and the main railway station every 20 mins: cost: 9 Euro. A taxi into the city centre costs around 50 Euro. The central information desk is on Level 3 *(Tel. 975 00).*

By car

Munich is well served by the German motorway network, with most links feeding directly into the central ring road (Mittlerer Ring).

By rail

Good rail links exist between major European cities. The main railway station (Hauptbahnhof) has links to almost all S-Bahn and U-Bahn (underground network) lines. Information: *Tel. 11 18 61; www.bahn.de*

INFORMATION IN MUNICH

Fremdenverkehrsamt
München [111 D4]
Mon–Thurs 9.30 am–3 pm, Fri 9.30 am–12.30 pm; 80331 München, Sendlinger Strasse 1; Tel. 089-233 03 00; Fax 23 33 02 33; www.muenchen-tourist.de

Tourist Information
Main railway station [110 A3]
Mon–Fri 9 am–8 pm, Sun 10 am to 6 pm; at south exit to Bayerstrasse; Tel. 089-23 33 02 57

Tourist Information
Marienplatz [111 D4]
Mon–Fri 10 am–8 pm, Sat 10 am to 4 pm; in New Town Hall

INTERNET

www.muenchen.de: general information on the city, e. g. travel, culture. *www.muenchen-tourist.de*: tourist information (both sites also in English).

INTERNET CAFÉS

One of the nicest is at Altheimer Eck. It seats 200, has 50 computers and reasonably priced Italian food. If you eat, you can surf for free, otherwise, you pay 3 Euro per hour. *Daily 11 am–1 am; Altheimer Eck 12; S- and U-Bahn: Marienplatz* [110 C4]

What does it cost?

Coffee	**2–2.50 Euro** a cup in a stand-up bar
Beer	**2.80 Euro** half a litre
Pretzel	**50 Cent** one pretzel
Food	**8–12 Euro** lunch
Bus ride	**2 Euro** single MVV ticket
Parking	**2.50 Euro** per hour

LOST PROPERTY

Municipal Lost Property Office: *Oetztaler Strasse 17;* [117 D5]; *Tel. 23 34 59 00; Mon–Fri 8 am–noon; Tues also 2 pm–5.30 pm; S- and U-Bahn: Hauptbahnhof.* For property lost at the main railway station: *Lost Property Office opposite platform 26* [110 A3]; *Tel. 13 08 66 64; daily 6.30 am–11.30 pm*

PUBLIC TRANSPORT

Single ticket 2, strip-card (ten strips) 9, day ticket 4.50; partner day ticket (up to five adults) 7.50 Euro (inner city). The München Welcome Card entitles the holder to free travel plus reduced admission at numerous museums and other sights, and on city tours. It is available at the tourist information offices at the main railway station and at Marienplatz. Information: *Münchner Verkehrs- und Tarifverbund GmbH*

(MVV); daily 6 am–10.30 pm; Tel. 41 42 43 44; www.mvv-muenchen.de

PASSPORT & VISA

Visas are not required for EU citizens; citizens of the USA or Canada require a visa only if staying for longer than three months. A valid identity card or passport is sufficient to allow entry into Germany.

POST & TELEPHONE

Post Office 32
(Main railway station) [110 A3]
Mon–Fri 7 am–8 pm, Sat 8 am to 4 pm, Sun 9 am–3 pm
Most post offices are open between 8 am and 6 pm. The international dialling code for Germany is 00 49. The area code for Munich is (0)89. From Munich, dial 0044 for Great Britain and 001 for the USA and Canada. Most public phones only take phonecards (5 Euro/10 Euro).

SIGHTSEEING TOURS

Gesellschaft für Münchner Stadtrundfahrten (Tel. 55 02 89 95): classic city tours. *Stattreisen München (Tel. 54 40 42 30; www.stattreisenmuenchen.de):* more unconventional programme. A comfortable and decidedly different alternative is a rickshaw tour (*Rikschamobil; Tel. 0171-287 30 32). Munich Bike & Walk Tours (Tel. 58 95 89 33; www.bikeandwalkcompany.de):* also with English-speaking guides.

TAXIS

Basic price: 2.50 Euro plus 1.30 Euro per kilometre. Per journey, an additional charge of 50 Cent is made, per item of luggage, a further 25 Cent. Radio taxi HQ: *Tel. 216 10*

TIME ZONES

Germany is six hours ahead of US EST and one hour ahead of GMT.

Weather in Munich

	Jan	Feb	Mar	Apr	May	June	July	Aug	Sept	Oct	Nov	Dec
Daytime temperatures in °C/F	1/34	3/37	9/48	14/57	18/	21/	23/	23/	20/	13/55	7/45	2/36
Night-time temperatures in °C/F	−6/21	−5/23	−2/28	3/37	7/45	10/50	12/54	11/52	8/46	4/39	0/32	−4/25
Sunshine: hours per day	2	3	5	6	7	7	7	7	6	4	2	1
Rainfall: days per month	11	10	9	10	12	14	13	12	10	9	9	10

Street Atlas of Munich

Please refer to the back cover for an overview
of this Street Atlas

Thanks to **holiday autos**
kein urlaub ohne

www.holidayautos.com

the totally relaxed way to start your holiday: exercise for beginners

1. make yourself comfortable and let your mind wander to the smart holiday autos prices and conditions. make it clear to yourself that holiday autos as the biggest intermediary for holiday rental cars in the world arranges you

   * rental cars in more than 80 holiday countries
   * at extremely attractive prices

2. now forget the usual extra charges and surprises, because thanks to

   * all-inclusive prices
   * elimination of the deductible
   * and third party liability insurance cover of at least € 1.5 million (usa: € 1.1 million)

   the price you actually pay is definite right from the start with holiday autos.

3. pick up the telephone very calmly, dial the number **0180 5 17 91 91** (12cents/min), surf to **www.holidayautos.com** or ask your travel agent about the tremendous offers made by holiday autos!

kein urlaub ohne

holiday autos

KEY TO STREET ATLAS

	Stadtgrenze · Gemeindegrenze Municip. boundary · Community bdry. Limite municipale · Limite communale		Fußgängerzone Pedestrian area Zone pietonne
	Bebauung · Öffentl. Gebäude Built-up area · Public building Terrain bâti · Bâtiment public	**26**	Straßenbahn (Tram) Tramway Tram
	Wald · Park Wood · Park Bois · Parc	**692**	Buslinie mit Haltestelle Bus with stop Autobus avec arrêt
	Sportplatz · Friedhof Sportsground · Cemetery Terrain de sport · Cimetière	**3,7m**	Max. Durchfahrtshöhe Max. clearance Tirant d'air max.
Kol.	Kleingarten · Industriegelände Allotment · Industrial area Jardins particuliers · Terrain industrielle	☗ ✝ ⚏	Kirche: evang./kath./sonst. Church: prot./cath./other Église: prot./cath./autre
20	Autobahn mit Anschlussstellennummer Motorway with number of junction Autoroute avec numéro d'echangeur	⊖ ⊜	Freibad / Hallenbad Open-air- / Indoor swimming pool Piscine en plein air / Piscine couverte
	Schnellstraße Expressway Route à plusieurs voies	◑ ◐	Polizei · Feuerwehr Police station · Fire station Com. de police · Poste des pompiers
471	Bundesstraße Primary route Route nationale	⊕ ⊟	Krankenhaus · Schule Hospital · School Hôpital · École
	Hauptstraße Main road Route principale	⬠ P·R	Parkhaus · Park & Ride Multi-storey car park · Park & Ride Bâtiment parking · Park & Ride
→	Einbahnstraße One-way street Voie à sens unique	⬠ ♟	Theater · Denkmal Theatre · Monument Théâtre · Monument

Symbols on the right denote barrier-free facilities

-Ⓢ-Ⓢ-	S-Bahn Suburban railway Train regional	o □	Öffentl. Telefon Public telephone Téléphone public
-Ⓤ-Ⓤ-	U-Bahn Subway Métro	(WC) WC	Öffentl. Toilette Public toilet Toilette publique
☻ ▽	Post Post office Bureau de poste	P P	Parkplatz Car park Parking

Scale 1:20.500-1:35.500
Hyperboloid projection with kilometre grid

	Marco Polo Walking Tours
1	Bargain-hunting
2	Architectural tour on wheels
3	Munich: Classic Bavaria

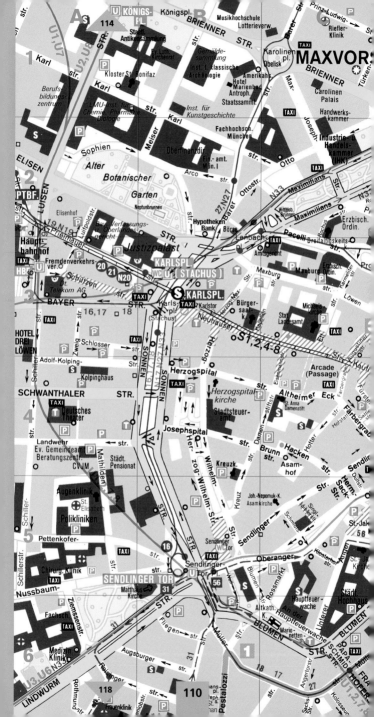

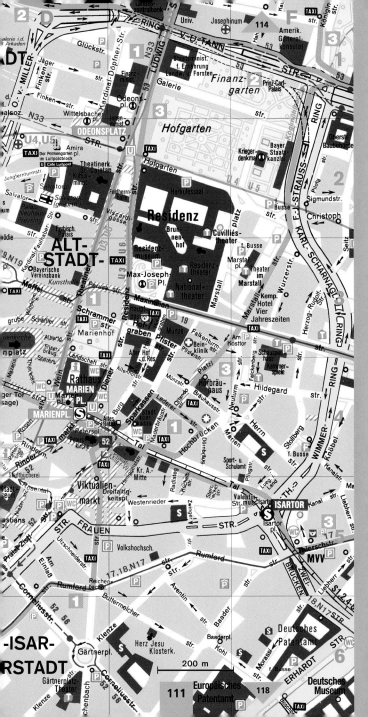

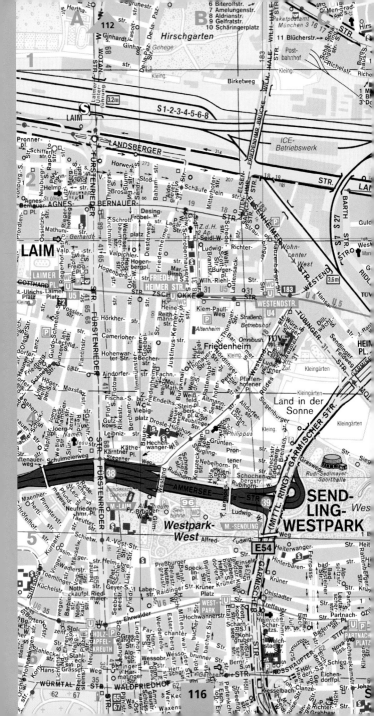

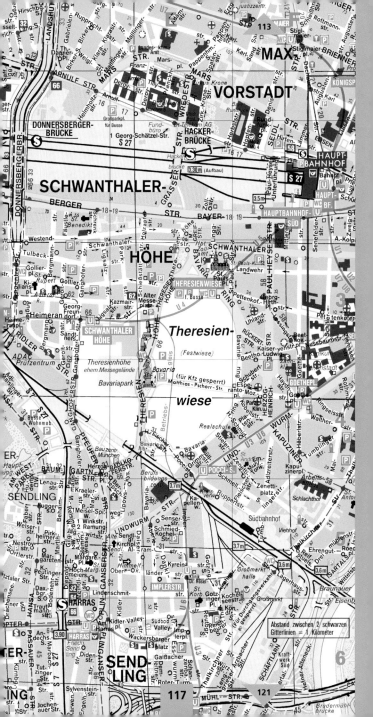

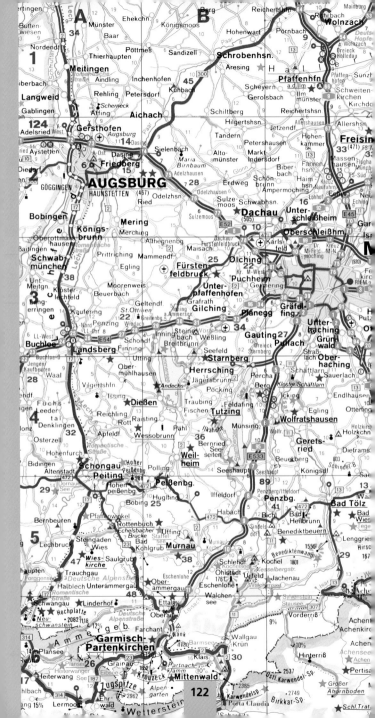

This index lists a selection of the streets and squares shown in the Street Atlas

A

Aberlestraße **117/E5-E6**
Ackermannstraße **113/F4-114/A3**
Adalbert-Stifter-Straße **115/F4-F5**
Adalbertstraße **114/B5-C6**
Adelgundenstraße **118/C3**
Adolf-Kolping-Straße **110/A4**
Agnes-Bernauer-Straße **116/A2-B2**
Agnesstraße **114/A5-B5**
Aidenbachstraße **120/A2-A4**
Aindorferstraße **116/A3-B4**
Ainmillerstraße **114/B4-C5**
Akademiestraße **114/C5**
Albertgasse **111/D3**
Albert-Roßhaupter-Straße **116/C6-117/D6**
Albrechtstraße **113/D5-E6**
Alexandrastraße **119/D2**
Allacher Straße **112/A2-B3**
Altenhofstraße **111/E4**
Alter Hof **111/E3-E4**
Altheimer Eck **110/C4**
Am Einlaß **111/D5**
Am Gasteig **119/D3-D4**
Am Gries **119/D1-D2**
Am Harras **117/D6**
Am Hirschanger **119/D1**
Am Isarkanal **120/C2-121/D2**
Am Kosttor **111/F3**
Am Lilienberg **119/D4**
Am Nockherberg **118/C5**
Am Perlacher Forst **121/E4-F4**
Am Westpark **117/D4-D5**
Amalienstraße **114/B6-C5**
Amiraplatz **111/D2**
Ampfingstraße **119/F4-F5**
An der Hauptfeuerwache **110/C6**
Angertorstraße **110/C6**
Anglerstraße **117/D3**
Anzinger Straße **119/E5-F5**
Arabellastraße **115/F6**
Arcisstraße **114/B5-118/A1**
Arcostraße **110/B2**
Aretinstraße **121/D3-E4**
Arnulfstraße **112/B5-117/F2**
Artur-Kutscher-Platz **115/F4**
Aschheimerstraße **119/F5**
Athener Platz **121/E4**
Auenstraße **118/A5-B4**
Auerfeldstraße **119/D5**
Auf der Insel **118/C3**

Augsburger Straße **110/A6-B6**
Augustenstraße **114/A5-118/A1**
Augustinerstraße **110/C3**
Authariplatz **121/E4**
Aventinstraße **111/E5-E6**

B

Baaderplatz **111/E6**
Baaderstraße **111/F5-118/B4**
Bad-Schachener-Straße **119/F5**
Bahnhofplatz **110/A3**
Balanstraße **119/D4-E6**
Baldeplatz **118/A5**
Baldestraße **118/A5**
Baldurstraße **112/B3-113/D3**
Barbarossastraße **119/F2**
Barerstraße **114/B5-118/B5**
Barthstraße **116/C2-C3**
Bauberger straße **112/A3-B2**
Bauerstraße **114/B4**
Baumgartnerstraße **117/D4**
Bavariastraße **117/E3-E4**
Bavariastraße **117/E4-E5**
Bayernplatz **114/A3-B4**
Bayerstraße **117/E2-118/A2**
Beethovenplatz **117/F3**
Beethovenstraße **117/F3**
Belgradstraße **114/B2-B4**
Berg-am-Laim-Straße **119/F4**
Bergmannstraße **117/D2-D3**
Berliner Straße **114/C3-115/D3**
Biedersteiner Straße **115/D3-D4**
Birnauer Straße **114/A2**
Bismarckstraße **114/C4**
Blumenstraße **110/B5-C6**
Blutenburgstraße **113/D6-E6**
Böhmerwaldplatz **119/F1-F2**
Bonner Platz **114/C3**
Bonner Straße **114/B3-C3**
Bordeauxplatz **119/E4**
Boschbrücke **111/F6**
Boschetsrieder Straße **120/A3-C2**
Bräuhausstraße **111/E4**
Breisacher Straße **119/E4**
Brienner Straße **111/D2-118/A1**
Brudermühlbrücke **121/D1**
Brudermühlstraße **120/B1-121/D1**
Bruderstraße **118/C2**
Bruggspergerstraße **121/E4**
Brundageplatz **113/F2**
Brunnerstraße **114/A3**

Brunnstraße **110/C4**
Bülowstraße **115/E6-F6**
Bürgerstraße **115/F4**
Burgstraße **111/E4**
Bürkleinstraße **118/C2**
Buschingstraße **119/F2**
Buttermelcherstraße **111/D5-E6**

C

Camerloherstraße **116/A3-B3**
Candidplatz **121/E1**
Candidstraße **121/E1-F1**
Christophstraße **118/C2**
Claude-Lorrain-Straße **118/B5-B6**
Claudius-Keller-Straße **119/E6**
Clemensstraße **114/A4-C4**
Corneliusbrücke **118/C4**
Corneliusstraße **111/D5-118/B4**
Crailsheimstraße **115/E2**
Crusiusstraße **119/D1-D2**

D

Dachauer Straße **112/A1-113/F6**
Daiserstraße **117/E5-E6**
Damenstiftstraße **110/B4-C4**
Danklstraße **117/E5-E6**
Dantestraße **112/C3-C4**
Danziger Straße **115/D3**
Delpstraße **119/F1-F2**
Demollstraße **112/C4**
Denninger Straße **115/E6-F6**
Destouchesstraße **114/A4-C4**
Dianastraße **119/D1**
Dienerstraße **111/D4-E3**
Dietlindenstraße **115/D3-D4**
Dietramszeller Straße **120/C1-121/D1**
Dom-Pedro-Platz **113/D4**
Dom-Pedro-Straße **113/D4-E4**
Donnersbergerbrücke **117/D2**
Dornbergstraße **119/F4**
Dreifaltigkeitsplatz **111/E5**
Dreimühlenstraße **118/A5**
Dultstraße **110/C4-C5**
Dürnbräugasse **111/E4**

E

Edlingerplatz **118/B5**
Eduard-Schmid-Straße **118/B5-C4**
Effnerplatz **115/F5-F6**
Effnerstraße **115/F4-F5**
Eggernstraße **119/D3**
Ehrwalder Straße **116/A6-B6**
Einsteinstraße **119/E3-F3**
Eintrachtstraße **119/D6**

Eisenmannstraße **110/C3-C4**
Elisabethplatz **114/B5**
Elisabethstraße **114/A4-B5**
Elisenstraße **110/A2-B3**
Elsässerstraße **119/E3-E4**
Elsenheimerstraße **116/B2-C3**
Elvirastraße **113/E6**
Emil-Riedel-Straße **119/D1**
Enhuberstraße **114/A6**
Erhardtstraße **111/F6-118/B4**
Erich-Kästner-Straße **114/B4**
Erich-Mühsam-Platz **114/C4**
Erzgießereistraße **113/E6-F5**
Esperantoplatz **117/F4**
Ettstraße **110/C3**
Europaplatz **119/D2-E2**

F

Fachnerstraße **116/B4**
Falckenbergstraße **111/F3-F4**
Falkenstraße **118/B5-C4**
Falkenturmstraße **111/E3**
Fallmerayerstraße **114/B4**
Färbergraben **110/C4**
Feilitzschplatz **114/C4**
Feilitzschstraße **114/C4-115/D4**
Feldmochinger Straße **112/C1-C2**
Fernpassstraße **116/C5-C6**
Filserbräugasse **111/D3**
Finkenstraße **111/D1**
Flemingstraße **115/F4-F5**
Fliegenstraße **110/B6**
Flurstraße **119/E3**
Frankfurter Ring **114/A1-115/E1**
Franziskanerstraße **119/D4-D5**
Franz-Josef-Strauß-Ring **111/F1-F2**
Franz-Joseph-Straße **114/B5-C5**
Franz-Mader-Straße **112/A3-B3**
Frauenlobstraße **118/A4**
Frauenplatz **110/C3-111/D3**
Frauenstraße **111/D5-F5**
Fraunhoferstraße **110/C6-118/B4**
Friedenheimer Brücke **116/B1-B2**
Friedenheimer Straße **116/B2-B4**
Friedenstraße **119/E5-D4**
Friedrichstraße **114/C4-C5**
Fromundstraße **121/F2**
Führichstraße **119/F5-F6**
Fürstenfelder Straße **110/C4-111/D4**

Fürstenrieder Straße
116/A2-A6
Fürstenried 118/B1

G
Gabelsbergerstraße
113/F6-114/B6
Galeriestraße 111/E1-F1
Galileiplatz 119/E1
Ganghoferstraße
117/D3-D5
Garmischer Straße
116/B6-C4
Gärtnerplatz 111/D6
Gedonstraße
114/C5-115/D5
Geiselgasteigstraße
120/C6-121/D3
Gelbsattelstraße
118/C4-119/D5
Georg-Brauchle-Ring
112/C2-113/F2
Georg-Elser-Platz 114/B6
Georgenstraße
114/A5-C5
Georg-Freundorfer-Platz
117/D3
Georg-Hirth-Platz 117/F3
Germaniastraße
114/C3-C4
Geroltstraße 117/D3-D4
Geschwister-Scholl-Platz
114/C6
Gewürzmühlstraße
118/C2-119/D2
Giesinger Berg 118/B6
Giselastraße 114/C5
Glückstraße 111/D1
Goetheplatz 117/D4
Goethestraße 117/F2-F4
Gollierplatz 117/D3
Gollierstraße
116/C3-117/E3
Görresstraße 114/A5
Gotthardstraße 116/A3
Grafinger Straße
119/E4-F5
Grasserstraße 117/E2
Greineberg 120/C2
Grillparzerstraße
119/E2-E3
Gröbenzeller Straße
112/B2
Grünwalder Straße
121/D4-F1
Grütznerstraße 119/D3
Guardinistraße 116/A6
Guido-Schneble-Straße
116/A3-A4

H
Habsburger Platz
114/C5
Hackenstraße 110/C4
Hackerbrücke 117/E2
Hahnenstraße 111/F1
Haidenauplatz 119/E3
Haimhauserstraße
114/C4-115/D4
Hanauer Straße
112/C3-113/D1
Hansastraße
116/C3-117/D6
Hans-Fischer-Straße
117/E4
Hans-Preißinger-Straße
121/D1
Hans-Sachs-Straße
118/B4
Härbelstraße 117/F4

Harlachinger Berg
121/D3
Harthauser Straße
120/C5-121/D4
Hartmannshofer Straße
112/A3
Hartmannstraße
110/C3-111/D3
Haydnstraße 117/F4
Hechtseestraße 119/F6
Heckenstallerstraße
120/A1-B1
Heiliggeiststraße
111/E4-E5
Heimeranplatz 117/D3
Heimeranstraße
117/D3-E3
Herkomerplatz 115/E6
Hermann-Sack-Straße
110/C5
Herrnstraße 111/F4
Herzog-Ernst-Platz
117/D4-D5
Herzog-Heinrich-Straße
117/F3-F4
Herzog-Max-Straße
110/B3
Herzog-Rudolf-Straße
111/F3
Herzogspitalstraße
110/B4-C4
Herzogstraße 114/A4-C4
Herzog-Wilhelm-Straße
110/B3-B5
Heßstraße
113/E4-114/B6
Hildegardstraße 111/F4
Hiltenspergerstraße
114/A3-A5
Himbselstraße 119/D2
Himmelreichstraße
119/D1
Hinterbärenbadstraße
116/C5-117/D5
Hirschgartenallee
112/A5-C6
Hochbrückenstraße
111/E4-F4
Hochstraße
118/C5-119/D4
Hofgartenstraße
111/E2-F2
Hofgraben 111/E3
Hofmannstraße
120/B2-B3
Hofstatt 110/C4
Hogenbergplatz
116/A3-B3
Hohenlohestraße
112/C4-113/D3
Hohenzollernplatz
114/A4-B4
Hohenzollernstraße
114/A4-C4
Holbeinstraße 119/E2
Holzhofstraße 119/D4
Holzstraße 118/A4-B4
Horemansstraße 113/D5
Hörwarthstraße 114/C3
Hotterstraße 110/C4
Hübnerstraße
113/D4-D5
Hugo-Troendle-Straße
112/B2-B3
Humboldtstraße 118/B5

I
Ichostraße 118/B6-C6
Ickstattstraße 118/B4
Ifflandstraße 115/D6-E5

Implerstraße
117/E5-120/C1
In den Kirschen
112/A3-B3
Infanteriestraße
113/F4-F5
Innere Wiener Straße
119/D3
Innsbrucker Ring
119/F4-F6
Isabellastraße
114/B4-B5
Isarring 115/D3-E5
Isartalstraße 118/A5
Isartorplatz 111/F5
Isenschmidstraße 121/D4
Ismaninger Straße
115/E6-119/D3
Isoldenstraße 114/C2-C3

J
Jägerstraße 111/D1
Jahnstraße 118/B4
Joergstraße 116/A3-A4
Johannisplatz 119/D3
John-F.-Kennedy-Brücke
115/E5
Josephspitalstraße
110/B4
Josephsplatz 114/A5
Jungfernturmstraße
111/D2

K
Kaiser-Ludwig-Platz
117/F3-F4
Kaiserplatz 114/C4
Kaiserstraße 114/B4-C4
Kanalstraße 111/F4-F5
Kapellenstraße
110/B3-C3
Kapuziner Platz 117/F4
Kapuziner Straße
117/F4-118/A5
Kardinal-Döpfner-Straße
111/D1-E1
Kardinal-Faulhaber-Straße
111/D2-D3
Karl-Müller-Weg
118/C3-C4
Karl-Preis-Platz 119/E5
Karl-Scharnagl-Ring
111/F2-F3
Karlsplatz 110/B3
Karlstraße
110/C2-117/E1
Karl-Theodor-Straße
114/A3-B3
Karmeliterstraße 110/C3
Karneidplatz 121/E3
Karolinenplatz 110/C1
Karolinenstraße 119/D1
Karolingerallee
121/D3-E3
Karwendelstraße 120/B1
Kaufingerstraße
110/C4-111/D4
Kaulbachstraße
114/C5-118/C1
Kazmairstraße
116/C3-117/E3
Kellerstraße 119/D4
Kidlerstraße 117/E5-E6
Kirchenstraße 119/E3
Kirchseeoner Straße
119/F6
Kißkaltplatz 114/C5
Klarastraße 117/D1-E1
Klausener Straße
121/F2

Klenzestraße
111/E5-118/B5
Klosterhofstraße 110/C5
Klugstraße
112/C4-113/D4
Knöbelstraße 118/C3
Kohlstraße 111/E6-F6
Kölner Platz 114/B3-C3
Kolosseumstraße 118/B4
Kolumbusplatz 118/B5
Kolumbusstraße 118/B5
Königinstraße
115/D5-118/C1
Königsplatz 110/B1
Kraepelinstraße 114/B2
Kreppeberg 120/C3
Kreuzplatz 118/C4
Kreuzstraße 110/B4-B5
Krüner Platz 116/B5
Krüner Straße
116/B5-C5
Küchelbäckerstraße
111/E4-E5
Kufsteiner Platz 115/E6
Kuglmüllerstraße
112/B4-C4
Kunigundenstraße
115/D3-D4
Kurfürstenplatz 114/B4
Kurfürstenstraße
114/B4-B5
Kurparkstraße 116/A5

L
Lachnerstraße 112/C5
Laimer Platz 116/A3
Lamontstraße 119/E1-E2
Landsberger Straße
116/A2-117/E2
Landschaftstraße
111/D3-D4
Landshuter Allee
113/D6-E1
Ländstraße 118/C3
Landwehrstraße
110/A4-117/F3
Laurinplatz 121/E4
Lautensackstraße
116/B2-B3
Lazarettstraße
113/E5-E6
Lechelstraße 112/A3
Ledererstraße 111/E4
Lenbachplatz 110/B2-B3
Leonhard-Moll-Bogen
116/C4-117/D4
Leonrodplatz 113/E4
Leonrodstraße
113/D5-E5
Leopoldstraße
114/C1-C5
Lerchenauer Straße
113/E1-114/A3
Lerchenfeldstraße
119/D1-D2
Leuchtenbergring
119/F3-F4
Liebfrauenstraße
110/C4-111/D3
Liebherrstraße 118/C3
Liebigstraße
118/C2-119/D2
Lilienstraße 118/C4
Lindenstraße
121/D4-D5
Lindwurmstraße
110/B5-117/E5
Lipowskistraße
117/E4-E5
Lothstraße 113/E6-F5

Löwengrube
110/C3-111/D3
Lucile-Grahn-Straße
119/E3
Ludwigsbrücke
118/C3-C4
Ludwigstraße
114/C6-118/C1
Lueg ins Land **111/F5**
Luisenstraße
110/A2-114/A2
Luitpoldbrücke (Prinz-
regentenbrücke)
119/D2
Luitpoldstraße
110/A2-A3

M
Maderbräustraße **111/E4**
Maffeistraße **111/D3**
Mailingerstraße
113/D6-E6
Mainzer Straße **114/C3**
Maistraße **118/A3-A4**
Mandlstraße **115/D4-D5**
Mangfallplatz **121/F3**
Mannhardtstraße **118/C3**
Marbachstraße **116/D6**
Margaretenstraße
117/D5
Maria-Einsiedel-Berg
120/C3
Maria-Einsiedel-Straße
120/C3
Maria-Hilf-Platz
118/C4-C5
Mariannenbrücke **118/C3**
Mariannenplatz **118/C3**
Mariannenstraße **118/C3**
Maria-Ward-Straße
112/A4
Marienplatz **111/D4**
Marienstraße **111/E4-F4**
Marsplatz **117/E1**
Marsstraße **117/D1-F2**
Marstallplatz **111/E3-F2**
Marstallstraße **111/F3**
Martin-Greif-Straße
117/E2-F2
Martin-Luther-Straße
118/B6
Mathildenstraße
110/A4-A5
Matthias-Pschorr-Straße
117/E4
Mauerkircherstraße
115/E6-F3
Max-Born-Straße
112/C1-113/D1
Maxburgstraße
110/B3-C3
Maximiliansbrücke
119/D3
Maximiliansplatz
110/C2-111/D2
Maximilianstraße
111/E3-118/C3
Max-Josef-Platz **111/E3**
Max-Joseph-Brücke
115/D6-E6
Max-Joseph-Straße
110/C1-C2
Max-Planck-Straße
119/D3
Max-Weber-Platz **119/D3**
Mazaristraße **111/D4**
Meilerweg **119/D3**
Meindlstraße
117/D5-D6
Meiserstraße **110/B1-B2**

Melusinenstraße
119/E5-F5
Menzinger Straße
112/A4-B4
Messeplatz **117/E3**
Metzstraße **119/D4-E4**
Miesingstraße **120/C3**
Milchstraße **119/D4**
Möhlstraße **119/E1-E2**
Montgelasstraße **115/E6**
Moosacher Straße
113/E1-114/A1
Morassistraße **111/F6**
Mozartstraße **117/F4**
Mühlbaurstraße
119/E2-D2
Mühldorfstraße
119/E4-F4
Müllerstraße
110/B6-111/D5
Münchener Freiheit
114/C4
Münzstraße **111/E4**
Murnauer Straße
120/A1-A2

N
Naupliastraße **121/E4-F3**
Nederlinger Platz **112/C4**
Nederlinger Straße
112/B3-C4
Neherstraße **119/E2**
Netzerstraße **112/B2-B3**
Neufriedenheimer Straße
116/A5-A6
Neuhauser Straße
110/B3-C4
Neumarkter Straße
119/F3
Neureutherstraße **114/B5**
Neuturmstraße **111/F4**
Nibelungenstraße
112/B5-C5
Nieserstraße **111/D5**
Nigerstraße **119/E2-E3**
Nikolaistraße
114/C4-115/D5
Nordendstraße
114/B4-B5
Nördliche Auffahrtsallee
112/B4-C4
Nördliches Schlossrondell
112/A4-B4
Normannenplatz **115/F5**
Notburgastraße **112/B5**
Nussbaumstraße
110/B5-117/F3
Nymphenburger Straße
112/C5-113/F6

O
Oberanger
110/B5-111/D4
Oberbiberger Straße
121/F3-F6
Oberföhringer Straße
115/E6-F4
Oberländerstraße **117/E5**
Obermaierstraße
118/C3
Odeonsplatz **111/E1**
Odinstraße **115/F5**
Oettingenstraße
115/D6-119/D2
Ohlmüllerstraße
118/C4-C5
Ohmstraße **114/C5**
Opitzstraße **115/F4**
Orlandostraße **111/E4**
Orleansplatz **119/E4**

Orleansstraße
119/D5-E4
Orpheusstraße **112/C3**
Oskar-von-Miller-Ring
111/D1-E1
Osterwaldstraße
115/D4-E2
Ottostraße **110/B2-C2**

P
Pacellistraße **110/C2-C3**
Papa-Schmid-Straße
110/C6
Pappenheimstraße
113/E6
Paradiesstraße **119/D1**
Pariser Platz **119/E4**
Pariser Straße
119/D4-E4
Partnachplatz **116/C6**
Parzivalplatz **114/C3**
Parzivalstraße
114/B3-C3
Passauer Straße
117/D6-120/B2
Paulanerplatz **118/C4**
Paul-Heyse-Straße
117/F2-F3
Paul-Heyse-Unterführung
117/F2
Pelkovenstraße
112/B2-113/D2
Perlacher Straße **121/F1**
Perusastraße **111/D3-E3**
Pestalozzistraße
110/B6-118/A4
Petersplatz **111/D4**
Pettenbeckstraße **111/D4**
Pettenkoferstraße
110/B5-117/F3
Petuelring **114/A2-C2**
Pfarrstraße **118/C2**
Pfeuferstraße **117/D4-D5**
Pfisterstraße **111/E3-E4**
Pflugstraße **111/F4-F5**
Pfrontener Platz **116/B4**
Pienzenauerstraße
115/E6-F4
Pilgersheimerstraße
118/B5-B6
Piusplatz **119/F5**
Platz der Freiheit **113/D6**
Platz der Opfer des
Nationalsozialismus
110/C1-111/D1
Platzl **111/E4**
Plinganserstraße
117/D6-120/C2
Poccistraße **117/E4**
Pognerstraße **120/C2**
Possartstraße **119/E2**
Potsdamer Straße
114/C3-115/D3
Prälat-Miller-Weg
111/E4
Prälat-Zistl-Straße
111/D5
Prannerstraße
110/C2-111/D2
Preßburger Straße
116/B5
Preysing Platz **119/D3**
Preysingstraße
119/D3-E3
Prielmayerstraße
110/A2-B3
Prinz-Ludwig-Straße
110/C1
Prinzregentenplatz
119/E2

Prinzregentenstraße
118/C2-119/F3
Professor-Huber-Platz
114/C6
Promenadeplatz
110/C3-111/D3
Pullacher Platz **120/C2**
Pütrichstraße
119/D3-D4

Q
Quellenstraße **118/C4**

R
Rablstraße **119/D4**
Radlkoferstraße **117/E4**
Radlsteg **111/E4-E5**
Raintaler Straße **121/F1**
Ratzingerplatz **120/A3**
Regerstraße **118/C5**
Reichenbachbrücke
118/B4
Reichenbachplatz
111/D5
Reichenbachstraße
111/D5-118/B4
Reinoltstraße **112/A3**
Reisingerstraße
110/A6-B6
Reitmorstraße
119/D1-D2
Renatastraße
112/C5-C6
Residenzstraße
111/E2-E3
Rheinbergerstraße
118/B1-C1
Rheinstraße **114/C3**
Richard-Strauss-Straße
115/F6-119/F2
Richard-Wagner-Straße
118/A1
Ridlerstraße
116/C3-117/D4
Riedlstraße **119/D1**
Riggauerweg **118/C4**
Rindermarkt **111/D4**
Ringseisstraße **118/A4**
Robert-Koch-Straße
119/D2
Rochusberg
110/C2-111/D2
Rochusstraße **110/C2**
Roeckleplatz **118/A5**
Romanplatz **112/B5**
Romanstraße **112/B5-C5**
Rondell Neuwittelsbach
112/C5
Röntgenstraße
119/E1-D2
Rosa-Luxemburg-Platz
113/E4
Rosenbuschstraße
119/D1
Rosenheimer Platz
119/D4
Rosenheimer Straße
118/C4-119/F6
Rosenstraße **111/D4**
Rosental **111/D4-D5**
Rossmarkt **110/C5-C6**
Rothmundstraße
118/A4
Rotkreuzplatz **113/D5**
Rottmannstraße
118/A1
Rückertstraße **117/F3**
Ruffinistraße **113/D5**
Rümannstraße
114/B2-C2

STREET ATLAS INDEX

Rumfordstraße
111/D5-F5
Rupert-Mayer-Straße
120/B3-C3
Rupprechtstraße **117/E5-F5**

S

Säbener Straße
121/F2-F4
Sachsenstraße
118/A6-B5
Salvatorplatz **111/D2**
Salvatorstraße **111/D2**
Sanatoriumsplatz **121/D4**
Sankt-Anna-Platz **118/C2**
Sankt-Anna-Straße
118/C2
Sankt-Bonifatius-Straße
118/C5-C6
Sankt-Ingbert-Straße
119/D6-E6
Sankt-Jakobs-Platz
110/C5
Sankt-Magnus-Straße
121/E3
Sankt-Martins-Platz
118/C6-119/D6
Sankt-Martin-Straße
118/C6-119/E5
Sankt-Paul-Straße
117/E3
Sankt-Quirin-Platz
121/F2
Sankt-Ulrichs-Platz
116/A3
Sattlerstraße **110/C4**
Schäfflerstraße **111/D3**
Schäftlarnstraße
117/F6-120/C2
Scheidplatz **114/B3**
Scheinerstraße **119/E1**
Schellingstraße
113/F5-114/C6
Schenkendorfstraße
114/C2-115/D2
Schillerstraße **110/A3-A5**
Schleibingerstraße
119/D4
Schleißheimer Straße
114/A1-117/F1
Schlosserstraße **110/A3**
Schmidstraße **110/C5**
Schneckenburgerstraße
119/E3
Schönfeldstraße **118/C1**
Schönstraße **121/D3-E1**
Schragenhofstraße
112/A3
Schrammerstraße
111/D3-E3
Schraudolphstraße
114/B5-B6
Schulstraße **113/D6**
Schüsselbergstraße
119/F4
Schützenstraße **110/A3**
Schwanthalerstraße
110/A4-117/E3
Schwarzstraße **118/C4**
Schweigerstraße **118/C4**
Schwere-Reiter-Straße
113/E4-F4
Schyrenplatz **118/B5**
Sebastiansplatz **111/D5**
Sedanstraße **119/D4-E4**
Seeaustraße **119/D2**
Seidlstraße **117/F1-F2**
Seitzstraße **118/C2**
Sendlinger Kirchplatz
117/E5

Sendlinger Straße
110/B5-111/D4
Sendlinger-Tor-Platz
110/B5
Senefelderstraße
117/F2-F3
Seybothstraße
121/D4-E4
Shakespeareplatz **119/E2**
Siebenbrunner Straße
121/D3
Siegenburger Straße
116/B4-C4
Siegesstraße
114/C4-115/D4
Siegfriedstraße **114/C4**
Siemensallee **120/A4-B4**
Siglstraße **116/B2-B3**
Sigmundstraße **111/F2**
Silberhornstraße
118/B6-C6
Simeonistraße
112/C4-113/D4
Simon-Knoll-Platz
119/D4
Singlspielerstraße **110/C5**
Sommerstraße
118/B5-B6
Sonnenstraße **110/B3-B5**
Sophienstraße
110/A2-B2
Soyerhofstraße
121/F2-F3
Sparkassenstraße
111/E3-E4
Spiridon-Louis-Ring
113/E3-F3
Sporerstraße **111/D3-D4**
Stachus **110/B3**
Steinbeisplatz **116/B4**
Steinheilstraße **114/A6**
Steinsdorfstraße
118/C3-119/D3
Steinstraße **119/D3-D4**
Stephansplatz **110/B6**
Stephansstraße **110/B6**
Sterneckerstraße **111/E5**
Sternstraße **119/D2-D3**
Sternwartstraße **119/E1**
Steubenplatz **112/B6-C6**
Stiglmaierplatz **113/F6**
Stollbergstraße
111/F3-F4
Straubinger Straße
116/B2-B3
Stubenvollstraße **119/D3**
Stuntzstraße **119/F2**
Südliche Auffahrtsallee
112/B5-C4
Südliches Schlossrondell
112/A5-B5

T

Tal **111/E4-F5**
Tassiloplatz **119/D5**
Tattenbachstraße **119/D2**
Tegelbergstraße
121/E3-F4
Tegernseer Landstraße
118/B6-C5
Tegernseer Platz **118/C6**
Tengstraße **114/A5-B4**
Thalkirchner Brücke
120/C2-121/D2
Thalkirchner Platz
120/C2
Thalkirchner Straße
110/B6-120/C2
Theatinerstraße
111/D3-E2

Theklastraße
110/C6-111/D6
Theodolindenstraße
121/D4-E4
Theodorparkstraße
115/D6
Theresienhöhe
117/E2-E4
Theresienstraße
114/A6-C6
Thiereckstraße **111/D4**
Thierschplatz **119/D2**
Thierschstraße
118/C3-119/D2
Thomasiusplatz **119/E6**
Thomas-Wimmer-Ring
111/F4-F5
Tierparkstraße **121/D3**
Tirolerplatz **121/E3**
Tivolistraße **115/D6**
Tizianplatz **112/B4**
Tizianstraße **112/B4-C4**
Trappentreustraße
117/D3
Treffauerstraße **116/C6**
Triebstraße **113/D1**
Triftstraße **119/D2**
Tübinger Straße
116/C3-C4
Tulbeckstraße **117/D3-E3**
Tumblingerstraße
117/F4-F5
Türkenstraße
114/C5-118/B1

U

Uhlandstraße **117/F3**
Ungererstraße
114/D4-E1
Unsöldstraße
118/C2-119/D2
Unterer Anger
110/C5-C6
Untermenzinger Straße
112/A2
Utzschneiderstraße
111/D5

V

Valleystraße **117/E6**
Valpichlerstraße
116/A3-B3
Veterinärstraße **114/C6**
Viktoriaplatz **114/C4**
Viktoriastraße
114/C3-C4
Viktualienmarkt **111/D5**
Virchowstraße
114/C3-115/D3
Viscardigasse **111/E2**
Vogelweideplatz **119/F3**
Volkartstraße **113/C5-E4**
Volpinistraße **112/B4-C4**
Von-der-Tann-Straße
111/E1-F1

W

Wackersberger Straße
117/E6
Wagmüllerstraße **119/D2**
Waisenhausstraße
112/C4-113/D5
Waldfriedhofstraße
116/A6-B6
Wallstraße **110/B5-B6**
Waltherstraße **118/A4**
Wartburgplatz **114/C2**
Washingtonstraße
112/C5-C6
Wedekindplatz **115/D4**

Weinstraße **111/D3-D4**
Weißenburger Platz
119/D4
Weißenburger Straße
119/D4-E4
Weißenfelderplatz
116/B4
Welfenstraße
118/C5-119/D5
Werdenfelsstraße **116/B6**
Werinherstraße
118/C6-119/E6
Werneckstraße
115/D4-D5
Westendstraße
116/B5-117/E2
Westenriederstraße
111/E5-F5
Westermühlstraße
118/B4
Wettersteinplatz **121/F1**
Widenmayerstraße
119/D1-D3
Wiener Platz **119/D3**
Wilhelm-Hale-Straße
112/C6-116/C1
Wilhelmstraße
114/C4-C5
Willi-Gebhardt-Ufer
113/D3-114/A3
Wilramstraße **119/E6-F6**
Winckelstraße **118/A4**
Windenmacherstraße
111/D3
Winfriedstraße **112/A6**
Winthirplatz **112/C5**
Wintrichring **112/B4-C2**
Winzererstraße
114/A3-A5
Wittelsbacherbrücke
118/A3-B5
Wittelsbacherplatz
111/D1-D2
Wittelsbacherstraße
118/A5-B4
Wolfratshauser Straße
120/A6-C3
Wörthstraße **119/D4-E4**
Wotanstraße
112/B5-116/A1
Wredestraße **117/E1**
Würmtalstraße **116/A6**
Wurzerstraße **111/F3**

Z

Zamboninistraße
112/B4-C4
Zaubzerstraße **119/E2-F2**
Zellstraße **119/D3**
Zenettistraße **117/F4-F5**
Zentnerstraße
114/A4-A5
Zentralländstraße
120/C3-C4
Zeppelinstraße **118/C4**
Zieblandstraße
114/A5-B6
Ziemssenstraße **110/A6**
Zillertalstraße
116/C6-117/D5
Zschokkestraße **116/B3**
Zuccalistraße
112/A5-A6
Zugspitzstraße **118/C6**
Zumpestraße
119/E2-E3
Zweibrückenstraße
111/F5-F6
Zweigstraße **110/A3**
Zwingerstraße **111/E5**

the totally relaxed way to start your holiday: exercise for advanced students

1. close your eyes and think very hard about the wonderful phrase "holiday rental cars for an all-inclusive price". remind yourself of all the many extras that are included in the price at holiday autos:

- unlimited mileage
- third party liability insurance with cover of at least € 1.5 million usa: € 1.1 million)
- comprehensive insurance without a deductible
- car theft insurance without a deductible
- all local taxes
- car provision at the airport
- airport charges

2. take a deep breath and consider the numerous awards holiday autos has won in recent years.

   you are not after all booking with any old company.

3. pick up the telephone very calmly, dial the number **0180 5 17 91 91** (12cents/min), surf to **www.holidayautos.com** or ask your travel agent about the tremendous offers made by holiday autos!

kein urlaub ohne

holiday autos

This index lists all sights, museums and destinations of outings featured in this guide. Numbers in bold indicate a main entry, italics a photograph.

Ägyptisches Museum 40
Alpines Museum **40**, 95
Alte Pinakothek 39, **40–41**, 45
Altes Rathaus 19–20
Altötting 99, **100**
Andechs 97, *99*
Architekturgalerie 93
Asamkirche **24**, *25*, 63
Bamberger Haus 29
Bavaria-Filmgelände 20
Bavarian State Mint 36
Bayerische Rück-versicherung 93
Bayerisches National-museum 39, **41**
Bernheimer Palace 35
Bernried 98
BMW-Hochhaus 93
BMW-Museum Zeithorizont 42
Botanischer Garten 27–28
Buchheim-Museum 98
Bürgersaalkirche 24–25
Burghausen 100
Centre for Unusual Museums 45
Chiemsee 101
Chinesischer Turm *12*, **28**, 51, 93
Climbing centre 32
Deutsches Jagd- und Fischereimuseum 42
Deutsches Museum 40, **42–43**
Dreifaltigkeitskirche 25
Easter Bunny Museum 45
Elisabethmarkt 33, **68**
Englischer Garten *7*, **28–29**, 32, *50*, 93, 95
Erding 29

Fashion Museum 45
Fernsehturm 8, **30**
Film and Photography Museum 45
Filmmuseum 83
Flugwerft Schleissheim *42*, **43**
Frauenkirche **25–26**, *94*
Fünf Höfe 66
Gärtnerplatzviertel 31
Gasteig 85
Gern 32
Glockenbachviertel 31
Glyptothek *38*, 39, **43**
Haidhausen 31–32
Haus der Kunst 28, 39, **43–44**, 95
Heiliggeistkirche 26
Herrenchiemsee *101*
Herreninsel 101
Herrmannsdorf 101
Herz-Jesu-Kirche 26
Hofbräuhaus 10, **60**, *90*, 95
Hofgarten 29
Hypohochhaus **20**, 93
Isartorplatz 34
Jagd- und Fischerei-museum 42
Karlsplatz **34**, *35*
Karlstor 34
Kleinhesseloher See 28, **29**, *50*
Kunsthalle der Hypo-Kulturstiftung 44
Kunstpark Ost 83
Lach- & Schiess-gesellschaft 82
Landshut 99–100
Lenbachhaus 39, **44**, 47
Lenbachplatz 34, **35**
Leopoldstraße 35–36

Ludwig-Maximilians-Universität **24**, 95
Ludwigskirche 26
Ludwigstraße **36**, 95
Luitpoldpark 29–30
Machtlfing 98
Marienplatz *6*, 11, **36**, 53, 94
Marstallmuseum 22
Mathildenbad 29
Maximilianeum **20–21**, 37, 94
Maximilianstrasse 11, **36–37**, *53*, 63, 94
Maxvorstadt 33
Michaelskirche 26
Monopteros 28
Mühltal 97
Müllersches Volksbad **21**, 95
Münchner Freiheit 10, 35, **37**
Münchner Stadtmuseum 44–45
Münsing 98
Musikhochschule 86
Museum Mensch und Natur 45
Nationaltheater **21–22**, 86, 94
Neue Pinakothek 39, **45–46**
Neues Rathaus **22**, 36, 53
Neuhausen 32
Nymphenburg *18*, **22**, 32
Oktoberfest 10, **14**, 16, 17, 65
Olympiagelände **30–31**, 93
Olympiapark 17, 19, 20, 29, **30**, 32

Pasinger Fabrik 86–87
Perfume Museum 45
Peterskirche *19*, **26–27**
Pinakothek der Moderne 39, 44, **46–47**
Pini-Haus 34
Porzellanmuseum 22
Prinzregententheater 86
Residenz 19, **23**, 95
Residenzmuseum 23, 39
Schlachthofviertel 33
Schlosspark Nymphenburg 19, **22**, 32
Schwabing **33**, 64, 91
Seeseiten 98

Seeshaupt 98
Sendling 33–34
Staatsgalerie Moderner Kunst 39, 44, **47**
Stachus **34**, *35*
St Anna im Lehel 27
Starnberg 97
Starnberger See *96*, 97
Strasslach 98
Südfriedhof 24
Theatinerkirche 19, **27**
Theatron 17, 19, 30
Therme Erding 29
Tierpark Hellabrunn 17, **31**
Tollwood 17
Tucherpark 93

Tutzing 98
Universität 24, 95
Valentin-Karlstadt-Musäum 34, 40, **47**, 94
Verwaltungsgebäude HYPO-Vereinsbank 20
Viktualienmarkt 16, 19, **68–69**, 91, 92
Villa Stuck 47
Vilsbiburg 99, 100
Völkerkundemuseum 39
Walking Man 35, 95
Wasserburg 101
Westend 34
Westpark 31, 32, ZAM 45

Get in touch!

Dear reader,

We make every effort to ensure you get the most up-to-date information available for your trip. Although our authors have done their research very carefully, errors or omissions do sometimes occur. We regret that the publisher cannot be held responsible for the consequences of such mistakes. We do, however, look forward to receiving your comments.

Please write to the editorial team at MARCO POLO Redaktion, Mairs Geographischer Verlag, Postfach 31 51, 73751 Ostfildern, Germany; or via e-mail: marcopolo@mairs.de

Picture credits

Cover photograph: Türme der Frauenkirche (HB Verlag)
Photos: Amberg: Schraml (96); Bilderberg: Madej (16); W. Dieterich (5 top, 6, 7, 14, 18, 28, 30, 35, 50, 56, 58, 60, 86, 92, 94); R. Freyer (front cover left, front cover centre, front cover right, 2 top, 4, 12, 49, 62, 63, 71, 78, 82, 87, 95, 102); R. M. Gill (61); HB Verlag (11, 21, 27, 48, 69, 99, 101, 107); Mauritius: Hackenberg (46); Mitterer (72); T. Stankiewicz (17, 19, 37, 42, 53, 54, 90); T. Widmann (1, 2 bottom, 5 bottom, 9, 20, 25, 38, 39, 44)

1st edition 2003 © Mairs Geographischer Verlag, Ostfildern, Germany
10th German edition
Editorial director: Ferdinand Ranft, Chief editor: Marion Zorn
Picture editor: Gabriele Forst, Editor English edition: Elke Arriens-Swan, Translator: Jane Riester
Cartography for the Street Atlas: © Mairs Geographischer Verlag/Falk Verlag, Ostfildern
Design and layout: red.sign, Stuttgart

Do's and don'ts

How to spare yourself trials and tribulations

Don't drive in Munich
Even if you've driven in Naples or Paris, leave your car in the hotel garage or on the edge of town (empty of luggage). Driving in Munich – especially during the rush hour – is like a fight to the death. Plus the fact that there are hardly enough parking spaces for the locals, so that you are practically forced to park illegally. Unfortunately, the overwhelming majority seems to see toughness and intransigence as the order of the day on the street. At traffic lights, they don't wait for green to drive off, and equally see amber as a sign to accelerate rather than slow down before the impending red light. Politeness only slows down the flow of traffic – or so those black sheep think who unfortunately seem to dictate the run of things. Illegal parking will cost you at least 15 Euro; if necessary, your car will be towed away, which means subsequent costs of up to 150 Euro.

Don't speak in dialect
Don't try to learn Bavarian. It is difficult enough to understand as it is. If you speak no German, it makes more sense to stick to English. On the other hand, if you fancy a bit of lingual gymnastics, have a few useful words at the ready for everyday use, such as 'Bitte' ('please'), 'Danke' ('thank you') and 'Wie viel kostet ...?' ('how much does ... cost?'). As for the local lingo, restrict yourself to 'Grüss Gott' for 'Good Day' and 'Pfiadi' for 'Goodbye'.

Don't criticise Munich
Don't go on to the locals about how much nicer, more comfortable and amusing it is in Berlin, London or New York. Remember, the people of Munich are entitled to run their city down as much as they like; tourists are expected to admire it unquestioningly.

Don't argue with the police
Don't go looking for trouble and argue with a policeman. Munich's custodians of the law are rated as fairly easy-going and even, in the case of minor misdemeanours, as lenient. If you remain calm and polite, you are more likely to get off lightly. If you attempt, however, to convince the policeman that the traffic light was under no circumstances whatsoever red when you drove through it, he'll have your driving licence faster than you can say Jack Robinson!

Don't look for 'genuine' folksiness
Unless you are fascinated by it, it's best to avoid such supposedly 'ethnic' places as the Hofbräuhaus or Munich's most Bavarian strip club, Die 'Schwarze Katz'.